How to Market, Advertise, and Promote Your Business or Service in Your Own Backyard

Tom Egelhoff

WILEY

John Wiley & Sons, Inc.

Library of Congress Cataloging-in-Publication Data:

Egelhoff, Tom.
  How to market, advertise, and promote your business or service in your own backyard / Tom Egelhoff.
       p. cm.
  Includes index.
  ISBN 978-0-470-25821-7 (pbk.)
 1. Small business–Management. 2. Small business–Marketing. 3. New business enterprises–Management. 4. Advertising. 5. Sales promotion. I. Title.
  HD62.7.E358 2008
  658.8–dc22

                                                                      2008002744

Printed in the United States of America.

10 9 8 7 6 5 4 3 2 1

He who finds a wife finds what is good
and receives favor from the Lord.
—Proverbs 18:22 NIV

To my best friend in the world—my wife Janet
For standing by me all these years and always having absolute faith in
me, when at times no one else did.

CONTENTS

FOREWORD

When Tom Egelhoff asked me to write the Foreword to his new book, I had no idea he was actually going to blame me for the whole project. However, while reading the Acknowledgment I discovered that he attributed the notion of writing a small town marketing book to a conversation we had several years ago. Although I don't remember having that conversation, and therefore can plausibly deny all responsibility for the end product, I was interested in reading the manuscript.

I can bluntly say, as a marketing professor for over 20 years, that this is the most practical and usable help for people to market small businesses in small towns that I've ever seen. By using lots of examples and talking in nontechnical language, Tom has made the secrets of marketing a business in a small town intellectually available to a wide audience. There are many good ideas here, even for folks with lots of experience.

As you read through the book, I would encourage you to apply the concepts to your business. While you'll find some outstanding ideas that you can apply immediately, the real benefit of the book will come from better understanding the perspective that is needed to successfully operate any business in the challenging environment of small towns. As Tom clearly points out, small towns typically don't provide a continuous flow of new customers. Tactics that will work successfully in larger cities often fail miserably in small towns. Market research data, information on the audience of media, demographic information, economic data, and a variety of other resources that can help guide decisions in more populated areas are typically sketchy or absent in smaller towns.

Despite this, small business owners make marketing decisions daily that can have substantial positive or negative impact. Prior to this book, there has been little in the way of guidance. I am very familiar with most of the academic and popular literature on marketing, and find little of it to be of much use for most of my small business consulting clients. The majority of it is too broad and general, and frequently describes tactics that may be appropriate for a large manufacturer, but difficult to translate to a small business scale.

Tom's book does an excellent job of adapting traditional marketing thought and technology to the unique problems of small towns. If you're marketing a small business in a small town, there is no better source of information available.

I intend to distribute this book to small town clients for whom I provide marketing consulting service. I think you'll find it to be helpful and informative.

—Mike Reilly
Professor of Marketing
Montana State University
Bozeman, Montana

PREFACE

Why You Need This Book

In my 40 years of dealing with small business owners, I've discovered that the way business is conducted is pretty much the same wherever in the world you happen to be. Business is nothing more than the exchange of value for goods and/or services provided by the business owner to the customer. The real business challenge is: What makes your backyard different from the other guy's backyard? Businesses are like fingerprints; no two are exactly alike. That's why a strong marketing and advertising plan will set you apart from everyone else.

I began writing about small business on my web site at www.smalltownmarketing.com in 1994. What amazed me most were the vast numbers of questions and e-mails I received from all over the world. It seemed that business was business, whether your backyard was in Bangor, Maine or Bangladesh. When I began looking for books that would help the small business owner with 10 or fewer employees, there wasn't much out there. As I searched for books specifically about marketing and advertising in a small town, I found none. So I decided to fill that void by writing the book you are holding.

This book is a 10-point, step-by-step guide to assist you in creating a marketing plan for your small business in your own backyard—that special little corner of your world where you take on all comers in the daily battle to keep your doors open and build a profitable, successful business.

Each point of the marketing plan builds on the previous point, and no point can be skipped. There is no such thing as "This point doesn't apply to my business." As you follow each of the steps, keep in mind that the ideas covered are designed to make you think and draw your own conclusions about the type of business you desire. How quickly or slowly do you want to grow? You will find techniques, examples, and ideas in this book that I've learned from business owners over the years that you might not have thought of when creating your own marketing plan.

There is an old saying, "The more things change, the more they remain the same." In the case of small business, I would modify the saying to: "The more things change, the more important the rules of marketing and advertising become."

For example, if you own a dry cleaning store in a large city, 80 percent of your customers might live within three or four blocks of your store. However, in a small town they may drive many miles from rural areas to get to you. The services you offer in the city might be entirely different than those you would offer in a small town.

Advertising options in a small town may be few, whereas in a large city there are many to choose from. But advertising in a large city is usually going cost more than in small towns, and mistakes can be very expensive.

Radio, television, and newspapers reach many more readers, listeners, and viewers in large cities than in smaller markets and cost more to produce. In a large city, does it make sense for our dry cleaner to advertise in the *New York Times*? A Sunday edition of the *Times* can have as many as 1,800 pages and weigh 12 pounds. The dry cleaner will certainly reach a lot of people, but are the millions reached ever going to show up at the business? The cost per thousand reached might be very attractive, but it's doubtful that people are going to travel clear across the city for dry cleaning no matter how good the cleaner or the ad is. If the dry cleaner is near people's workplace, then they might go there instead of to one near their home, and that could account for the other 20 percent of the store's business.

The next question would be: "Is this true of all businesses?" The answer is a resounding no. It's definitely not true of all businesses. At least it's not true for those business owners who use creative marketing techniques to rise above their competition.

Some people will travel great distances to certain types of businesses. For example, Rodeo Drive in Beverly Hills, California, attracts not only the rich and famous but tourists from all over the world as well. More important, certain kinds of advertising and marketing messages will draw people from far away.

Coin Mart Jewelers, in Chula Vista, California, ran a very creative ad campaign years ago that didn't advertise jewelry or coins or any other products. The ad campaign simply said that if you came to Coin Mart with a piece of plain white paper, they would show you how to know you were getting a real diamond and how to tell its value. According to the ads, providing the information would take about 45 minutes.

Purchasing a diamond, even a small one, is a major expense for most people. Would it make sense to drive a few extra miles to Coin Mart and get educated about a diamond's value? You would still have the option of buying from a local neighborhood jeweler, right? Or would the chances be high that while you were at Coin Mart and in the market (why else would you be there?), you just might find the diamond you want and buy it?

Coin Mart found a way to increase its selling area in a way that would justify the purchase of advertising that would cover all of the

San Diego area, or about seven million people. The ads would also reach a more affluent target market. They sold the value of education and trust first, which in turn would lead to the sale. Now, would this campaign work today?

It would probably not be as effective because of the Internet. A buyer could find thousands of pages on how to tell the value and quality of a diamond. But this type of campaign might produce enough customers to pay for itself, and that's the objective of any advertising. It must produce more sales than it costs.

And this brings me to the next reason why you need this book. Almost every aspect of marketing and advertising is different for small markets in bigger cities compared to small businesses in small towns. Target markets are different, as are cultures and traditions, ethnic makeup, local and state government regulations, licensing—the list is endless.

The biggest difference is population within the profitable distance of your business. For example, in New York City you are looking at 27,000 people per square mile. In Montana there are only six people per square mile. Reaching these two completely different markets requires totally different tactics even though the businesses might be strikingly similar.

What does "profitable distance" mean? If you are a carpet cleaner, there is a certain distance you can't go beyond and still make a profit on the job.

Time and distance will determine if a job is profitable. In a larger city, there are so many people crammed into such a small footprint that you may never have to travel more than a few miles to complete enough jobs to make your business profitable. Even if you have several competitors, the sheer number of customers can still keep you in business.

In the case of a small or rural market, where the population is sparse, both you and your competitors have to travel further on each job than your big city counterpart, just to service your market.

The small town carpet cleaner will have a smaller customer base just because of the smaller population base. Although each carpet cleaner does basically the same job, the geographic and demographic market for each can be dramatically different.

So how can you set yourself apart in your own backyard? Most of the things I know about business I learned from my father—not so much the nuts and bolts of day-to-day business operation, but watching the respect my father received from both customers and the community at large because of the way he did business. In order for that to happen, you have to be a particular kind of person.

My father ran his life, and his business, in an ethical and professional manner. One of the things I try to stress in this book is that there are no shortcuts in ethics and professionalism. You show professionalism every day, and every day a few more people see it and report it to others. The days of manipulating or taking advantage of the uninformed customer are quickly coming to an end. If you have been conducting your business in an unethical manner, your days in business are numbered.

Due to the Internet, customers in all markets are more informed than ever, and they will be even more informed in the future. It is imperative that every person in your business be an expert in product knowledge. Even obscure brand names are no longer beyond the reach of your customers.

Customers today simply can't be permitted to walk through your door and be better informed about your products and services than you are. If this happens, you are going to be a victim of the on-line sales juggernaut of customers looking to save money by eliminating the uninformed middleman whom they see no real need to consult.

Customers need to feel that, although they have done their research and know the kinds of products they are looking for, there is still the need to deal with an expert in the field in order to get the best deal possible. The more they have vested in the deal, the more likely they are to defer to your expertise, and this confidence in you will lead to more and larger purchases in the future.

This is where the vast majority of small businesses, in both large and small markets, drop the ball. According to the Small Business Administration, 85 percent of all small businesses fail in the first five years. Business is built on feelings and emotions. How do I feel about dealing with you? How do I feel about your products? How does your product make me feel?

Customers don't buy features. They buy the *benefits* of the products or services you sell. Marketing finds the customer's hot button, and the advertising message pushes it. Only businesses on the downhill slide to oblivion sell their products' features; successful businesses that stand the test of time sell benefits to their customers.

In the chapters ahead I will cover these and other topics in greater detail for businesses of any size, anywhere in the world, because business challenges are universal. Even though the view or the language may vary, there are few variables between most successful business owners. They have learned to become students of their industries, and they know how to find customers and how to present value. They are both ethical and professional in every aspect of their business. If you would like to join this very select group, then read on.

ACKNOWLEDGMENTS

V ery special thanks to Professor Mike Reilly, of the marketing department of Montana State University, for writing the foreword and for encouraging me to jump into the deep end of the pool and write this book.

Mike and I met while presenting a marketing seminar in Bozeman, Montana, to a convention of Montana educators in 1993. I had recently moved to Bozeman. At lunch I mentioned to Mike that I had been toying with the idea of writing a small business marketing newsletter.

Mike, in the special style he has, pointed out that a newsletter was a lot of work. "Why don't you just write a specialized book on marketing?" he suggested. Sure, just write a book ... about what? Marketing has been done to death and, besides, who would read a book written by me?

The introductory Small Town 101 chapter of this book details how I was inspired to write about small town marketing. I hope you enjoy it.

INTRODUCTION

Small Town 101

The Miracle Mile

This book was conceived, in part, because of a Powerball lottery winner and a Rand McNally Road Atlas. You may remember the name Leslie Robins—the teacher who won the first $110 million Powerball lottery. It seems that Robins lives within walking distance of a lottery winners' "miracle mile" in Fond du Lac, Wisconsin.

This miracle mile has produced more than $150 million in winners. Upon reading this rather interesting article, I pulled out the Rand McNally to see exactly where this town is located. When I reached the map of Wisconsin, I was amazed to discover that there are so many small towns there that their names barely fit within the borders of the state.

After finding the miracle mile, I quickly decided not to jinx those already living there by packing up the wife and moving to Fond du

Lac. Instead, I continued to look through the Rand McNally to see if other states had similar numbers of small towns. To my surprise, many did not. California, for example, is the most populous state in the country, but it has a much lower ratio of small towns to large ones than, say, Illinois or Missouri. Eastern Kansas has many towns; western Kansas, relatively few. My home state of Montana has its highest concentration of towns in the western portion of the state.

Okay, so what? Every state has a higher number of small towns than large cities, and what difference does it make where they're located? Well, the size of the town, and how it is located in relation to larger cities, can have a great influence on your business success or failure.

How Small Towns Work

Let me use my own hometown of Bozeman, Montana, as an example. In larger cities throughout the nation, goods and services are available in large numbers. If you want carpet for your home, just open the yellow pages and there are many to choose from.

In a small town the choices are more limited. If there is a large city nearby, I need to make a decision. Is it worth it to me to travel to the big city to make my purchase? If so, what about service? Will the big city company come all the way out to my little town if I have a problem? Will there be a service charge due to the distance? How much service will I need, and is it worth it? Are the savings, if any, worth the drive?

Drive a Lot, Save a Little?

Bozeman is a town in southwestern Montana with a population of 32,600; during the summer the town shrinks to 22,000 because Montana State University is not in session. The nearest sizable city to the west is Butte, 82 miles away, population about 37,000. To the east is Billings, 142 miles away, population about 90,000, the largest city in Montana. Do people make the long drives from Bozeman to shop in these cities? Believe it or not, they often do!

Before you question the sanity of Montanans, keep in mind that distances in Montana are perceived differently than in other areas of the country. With 147,000 square miles and a population of only 900,000 people (that's six people per square mile), the freeways are virtually empty by most big city standards. This makes the drive a family outing, and the scenery on the way to Butte or Billings is, to say the least, spectacular.

Many businesspeople must travel to these cities to meet with manufacturers and suppliers. It's the only way they can do certain types of business. The point I want to make is this: In a small town there is isolation, and that can be very good for business.

If you have the goods and services customers want and they feel they can do business with you, they will not make that drive, regardless of how beautiful it is. Best of all, in a small town the amount of competition is reduced. However, if you don't manage your business effectively, everyone in town may well drive down the road to the bigger city.

Now, what about small businesses in a big city? What are their options? The city has a larger concentration of customers, which will attract more competition. The bigger the customer base, the more businesses that base can support. But you can almost always count on the 80/20 rule. Twenty percent of the bakeries will do 80 percent of the bakery business in a given area. The big question is: Will you be in that 20 percent?

The Social Graces

Another important point to keep in mind is that small towns are more socially oriented than large cities. You know not only your next-door neighbor, but probably everyone on your block, including all the kids. There are positives and negatives to this.

On the positive side, many neighborhoods treat new arrivals as a great excuse to have a party. Cakes and cookies are baked, cookouts are organized, and a block party breaks out. These are the people who will help you ease into your new business environment. They will be happy to take you to their service clubs, introduce you at church functions, and help you fit in.

The flip side is that some areas of the country see newcomers as meaning weird accents, strange dress, more crime, more traffic, higher housing prices, more government, and the deterioration of their once peaceful village—forgetting all the while that at one time they may have been new in town themselves. Some of these people will have to be won over. Here are seven suggestions on how to do just that:

1. Find the friendliest person in town and build on him or her. In small towns, these are the folks you hear about most. Many are mentioned in the newspaper or on local television on a regular basis. In larger cities there is always a neighborhood business leader. He or she may be the head of the economic development group or the local chamber of commerce. Invite these folks to lunch and ask them to introduce you to your new neighborhood.

2. Be positive about your new home. Negative comments about your new town or neighborhood will not be well received. Whether you moved from a small town to a big city or vice versa, you did so for a reason. Don't expect your new home to adapt to you—you must adapt to it.

3. Don't tell people how good everything was in your previous hometown. You may be invited to go back. If everything was so perfect, why did you leave? Remember all the reasons you moved. Look forward, not backward.

4. Learn as much about the town as possible before you move, so you can take part in local conversations. Subscribing to the local

newspaper is a good source of information. However, it's not a good idea to quote the newspaper on an issue. Although nearly everyone reads the paper, few will admit the paper fairly represents their side of any issue.

5. Avoid talking about politics or religion until you know your listeners well. Find ways to get involved in the community as soon as possible. Join clubs such as the Rotary, Kiwanis, Lions, and Elks. Attend the church of your choice regularly and introduce yourself to as many people as possible. (It's not the purpose of this book to espouse any religious ideology, but in my opinion, church is the most nonthreatening place in any town, big or small, to make friends. Its purpose is to welcome you into the fold and help you.)

6. Join your local chamber of commerce. If you have special skills, make sure they know about you. Every day people contact the chamber for recommendations for various goods and services.

7. Can you teach your skill? Contact the nearest adult education organization. They are always on the lookout for qualified business experts. I teach classes in web site marketing, sales, computer layout, marketing and advertising, and business card and brochure design. Each of these classes has led to business contacts and jobs. I also make valuable business contacts with class members, whose expertise and contacts in their specific areas can be valuable to me in the future. The best rule is: You can't know too many people.

Expertise: Have You Got It?

If you've owned or managed a business in an urban area, the chances are you will have a higher level of expertise in your field than most of your local peers who have not operated a business in a large city. Before those of you who own a business in a small town throw this book across the room, let me explain that statement in more detail.

I don't mean to imply that just because you have a business in a small town you don't know what you're doing. There are plenty of very successful business owners in small towns. This book chronicles the ideas of many of them. It's just a simple fact—there are certain advantages in larger cities that just aren't available in smaller towns.

Let me use a sports analogy to explain my position. The tougher the competition, the better a team becomes over the long haul. The very fact that tough competition exists forces a business owner to get tough and lean, or cease to exist. Wal-Mart puts small businesses to the test every day across the country. Its buying power and advertising clout have put many a small town operation out of business. However, in many cities, business owners have learned how to compete against the powerful big box stores and continue to operate thriving businesses.

The level of competition is almost always higher in larger cities. There are more stores providing the same goods and services at very competitive prices. The employee pool is larger and more experienced. The advertising options are more extensive. The promotional opportunities are better. The successful business owner can quickly learn marketing secrets from some very talented people who don't make a lot of mistakes.

Does this mean that if someone from a big city opens a business, you should close yours? Of course not. An established business will always have some advantage over a new one, unless the newcomer is a national chain or well-known name that can generate a quick customer base.

Learn the Ways of a Tiger

So, how should I compete against all this expertise? Well, you could move your business to a major city for a couple of years, and then move it back again. A better idea might be one a college professor taught me, and it's very simple: "To catch a tiger, learn the ways of a tiger." In other words, learn as much as you can about your business, your competitors, and your customers.

One of the best places to find industry information is a trade magazine. Often when I read about a marketing consultant in a business magazine, I would call the person, and we would talk as long as he or she would stay on the phone. I remember talking with a business consultant in Hawaii for over two hours. The expense of the phone call was a small price to pay for the knowledge I received.

Another great way to get information is by talking to salespeople who call on you. Remember, they also sell to your competitors, and may let valuable information slip during casual conversation.

Business today calls for more and more expertise. One thing is certain: Small town or large, knowledge is power.

Knowledge Is Power

Read as much as possible about your profession. Will Rogers once said, "All I know is just what I read in the papers." And he made a living telling it to audiences around the world.

Subscribe to as many trade magazines as you possibly can, and take time to read them. Many are free to qualified companies. You may say, "I don't have the time to do all the things I need to do now, let alone read magazines." Well, that's okay—when your business fails you'll have plenty of time to read. Find the time now.

If you spend 20 minutes a day reading something about your industry, at the end of one year you will know more than 75 percent of the people in that industry know. Find, and talk to, a knowledgeable expert in your industry at least once a month. Learn the ways of a tiger.

Now let's get started creating your marketing plan.

CHAPTER 1

The Small Town Marketing Plan

Getting Started

Now that we've established a small town perspective with the Small Town 101 section, let's look at the parts of the marketing plan, and how to use each one.

What is a marketing plan, anyway? You may be saying, "I thought I just needed a business plan." A marketing plan is part of your overall business plan. I usually recommend that 30 percent of your business plan should be devoted to how you are going to market your business. Your marketing plan is one major area that investment bankers take a very close look at before lending you any money. They are very curious to know how you plan to attract customers, make sales, make a profit, and pay back their investment in your business.

You will use some of the information from the business plan in your marketing plan, but the marketing plan is usually its own entity within the business plan. If you don't have a business plan started, begin assembling the information today.

SCORE, "Counselors to America's Small Business," offers free help to get you started. You will find a free business plan template at www.score.org. If there isn't a SCORE office near you, the organization has over 1,000 counselors available online. Find them by asking your local chamber of commerce or checking the SCORE web site.

Also, check out your local Small Business Development Center (SBDC). The local SBDCs are part of the Small Business Administration and are prepaid with your tax dollars. You can find the nearest office at www.sba.gov (or Google "SBDC," followed by your state). These offices are in most large cities throughout the United States.

If you are in a smaller town that lacks these advisory groups, create your own set of coaches by taking retired or local business leaders out for coffee. Pick their brains in a methodical manner. These are the people who have successfully done what you want to do and made a profit doing it. Their experience and expertise can save you hundreds, even thousands of dollars in mistakes you might have made without their advice.

The last part of your business plan will deal with your financial condition. These numbers are critical to your business success. If you are anything like me, you are definitely not a numbers person. A balance sheet, profit and loss statement, and cash flow projections are financial information that banks are going to want to see before giving you a loan.

Where do you start, and how can you predict sales figures for something you've never done before? If you are unsure of how to arrive at these numbers, SCORE and your local Small Business Development Center can help you put the numbers together. They have ratios of how much a landscaping business or a day care center should make in its first year. They can give you industry norms on the percentages certain types of businesses spend on advertising, inventory, and payroll. The online SCORE business plan outline or template, mentioned earlier, contains Excel spreadsheets, complete with formulas. Just fill in the blanks, and it will do the math for you. When you have your financial statements and projections completed, you can move on to the marketing plan.

Where do we start?

We start with you. You must sit down and really look at yourself, and your business, as you never have before. This is the most difficult part of the marketing plan. We never let anyone really see the real us. You must be completely honest with yourself about who you are, and where you're going.

A Little Information Is a Dangerous Thing

Before customers enter into a relationship with a business, quite naturally, they want to know something about that business. That's where a marketing plan starts. Who are you? Why would customers want to do business with you? In addition, you need to know every aspect of your business before you can prepare your advertising and target those customers. Here's how to start.

If you were looking for a job and saw an ad in the classifieds, what questions would you ask yourself? The first question would probably be: "Am I qualified to do this job based on the job description?" If the answer is yes, you put together a resume and request an interview to present your qualifications to your prospective employer.

Business operates in a similar manner. You need a complete description of your business (business resume) that can be presented to qualified customers (your potential employer) in the form of an advertising message that will cause them to buy your products (hire you).

The next chapter covers the types of things that should be included in your business resume.

CHAPTER 2

Step 1: Business Resume: Who Are You?

Resume Background Questions

Ask yourself the following 11 groups of questions as though you were a customer of your business. (The first three groups of questions are from the customer's viewpoint.) Warning: Do not skimp or gloss over this business resume section. It will be very valuable later, when we deal with positioning your business.

1. How long have you been in business? If you are a new business, what experience do you have in this field? As a customer, would I feel comfortable that you can do the job or provide the level of service I am accustomed to? Are specialized machines needed in the production of your product? Could the need to import materials put the company in jeopardy if they weren't available? Is your industry market share

growing or shrinking? Will training be required for employees to produce the products? What are the company's long- and short-term goals? Are there existing sales goals? What is your mission statement or company philosophy?

2. Who are the principals in your business? What qualifies them to start or operate this business? What special skills do they have? What is their education or training in this industry? Are they members of any industry associations? Have they received any awards or certificates that certify their expertise? Is city or state licensing required for this business, and, if so, have they complied with all local, state, and federal regulations?

3. What purchase rates or buying habits are related to your product or service? Would I buy it once a week, a month, or a year? What is the demand for your product or service? Is it seasonal? Is it hard to use? Are there multiple users? Are there going to be heavy users? Does it require maintenance or repair? What percentage of your total sales will they be? Is your industry growing or shrinking? Is the customer base in your selling area growing or shrinking? Is your product a luxury or a necessity?

4. Are people even aware your product exists? Do they have preconceived impressions of your product or service? Is your product harmful to the environment? Is it fun or useful? Will you need a patent, trademark, or copyright? Is your product well known, or will the public need to be educated about how to use it? Is it the next hula hoop or pet rock?

5. Most businesses have some form of competition—how about yours? Who is your principal competition? (Re-ask all the questions in #2 about each of your competitors.) How big are your competitors? What can you do that they can't or won't do? Can you specialize in areas they can't? If you are competing against a large public company (e.g., Wal-Mart, Costco, etc.), buy some of its stock. You'll receive the annual report, and as a stockholder, a lot of information will be available to you.

6. How's your pricing compared to the competition? Can you be competitive, or are you going to have to ask a higher price? Is the lowest price always the best? Of course not. Customers place a value on products based on their perceptions of that product. They base those perceptions on the information they receive from you, other sources, and comparisons. If I say, "CD player," a dollar figure jumps into your head based on advertising you've seen, input from friends, or any one of a hundred different sources.

7. You can't have a business without customers. You must identify your target market as narrowly as humanly possible. Who are the people most likely to use your business? Their age? Sex? Occupation? Marital status? Home ownership? Television shows they watch? Newspapers and magazines they read? Average household income? Education? Lifestyle? Number of children? Dog or cat owner? (All the items you might find on a warranty card when you purchase a vacuum cleaner or blender.) In addition, do some secondary research. For example, if you are lucky enough to be in a town large enough to have a public library, it should have census information for your state and county. If not, look it up on the Internet at www.census.gov. This will give you a profile of the average person living in your town and county.

The chamber of commerce may have the demographics of your town. Start with these and be prepared to adjust your business as needed. A good library will have a copy of the *Rand McNally Commercial Atlas and Marketing Guide.* You'll find retail sales data for your state and county. What did people spend on food? Housing? Clothing? Automobiles? It's a great thumbnail source of information about people in your state or county. I cover how to reach these folks in the advertising section, coming up later in the plan.

Who are the end users of your product? For example, if I ask my wife to pick up some beer when she goes to the store, she makes the purchase, but she is not the end user of the product; I am. If I recommend a brand name, I influence the purchase; if not, she will probably get something light or on sale.

8. How much business is really out there? In a small town, this information becomes very important. I grew up in a small farm town in southern Illinois. The population was 5,200, yet in a three-block area there were six gas stations. These stations all stayed in business during my elementary to high school years. That's a minimum of 12 years in business. When you create your business plan, you must know if there are going to be enough paying customers to support your business.

Forget the competition (not entirely) for the moment. Each of those gas stations had to service a large enough share of the 5,200-customer base to survive in that market. Some customers went to only one station during all 12 years; some went to all of the stations during the 12 years; and the rest were between the two extremes. The point is, each station needed X number of regular customers per day, week, month, and year to survive.

Could a seventh station go into this market and survive? The answer is yes. Would it be easy? The answer is no. If you were going to open a new gas station in this market, you would need to know the answers to the following three questions:

1. Can you develop new customers who do not currently go to any of the other stations? (There might be new people moving to town, or young people just turning 16 and getting a driver's license.)

2. Can you take customers away from your competitors? (There are always customers who are unhappy with the service, the quality of the product, or the price.) Are there competitor weaknesses you can exploit?

3. Can you develop enough of both types of new customers to make a living?

If the answer to each of the three questions is yes, I would advise you to continue constructing the marketing plan. But please keep in mind we are only in step 1 of a 10-step plan. This gas station example is greatly simplified for demonstration purposes. There are a lot more things that have to happen for that seventh gas station to survive than just those three questions. But if the answer is no, then I would advise you to stop and regroup.

This process is commonly called a sales and market share analysis. How many sales and how many customers are needed for the business to survive? I will tackle this in more detail as we go through the rest of the marketing plan.

9. Next, let's talk about how you will get your product to your customer. What is your service area? The whole town? The state? The country? The world? Is it delivered? Do customers pick it up? Can or does it need to be shipped? Will you need delivery vehicles? A shipping budget? FedEx account? UPS? Is it an intangible or service item such as life insurance, office cleaning, or dog grooming? Do customers come to your place of business, or do you go to their home or business? In small towns or rural areas, you may be required to travel for business. How much travel will be necessary, and what is the cost?

10. How is the product or service going to be sold? Where do customers shop for your product now? Will this change in the future? Will you need to hire salespeople? Will it be sold off the shelf in retail stores? Mail order? Internet? 800 number? Do you know what the cost of sales of the product or service will be? If you have to pay a commission to a salesperson, how will you determine the commission percentage?

11. If you are in a common industry, like shoe stores, construction companies, CPAs, real estate, and so on, start studying how these companies are advertising in your area. Are they on radio? Television? Newspapers (what section and what days)? In San Diego, construction and remodeling companies comprise almost all the ads in the weekly newspaper TV listings. Why? Because that part of the paper is the one section that hangs around the house all week.

Customer Service

The last area of the business resume that I want to cover is customer service. Why even bother to mention customer service? Shouldn't it be a given to deliver the best customer service possible? Every book says, "Knock their socks off," "Wow 'em," "Blow the doors off," "Exceed every expectation." But is this really the kind of service you want to deliver? Let's look at customer service in more detail, and you might change your mind.

Defining Customer Service   What is your definition of customer service? Do you think mine is exactly the same as yours? Would my wife's be different from both of ours? The problem with customer service is its definition and how that definition fits within your business.

We all know bad service when we get it. But is that service bad for everyone? Some people are more temperamental than others. Some customers want over-the-top attention, whereas others just want what they came in for, and are out the door. So, if we are to assume that each customer is different, how can we define our customer service so it fits everyone? Let me define customer service for you; then I'll explore who delivers it and why.

In the movie *The Man Who Shot Liberty Valance*, the Jimmy Stewart character debunks a long-held legend about who really shot the famous outlaw. The newspaper interviewer decides not to use Stewart's account, saying, "When the truth conflicts with the legend, print the legend."

I mention that movie because there is a famous story about Nordstrom department stores. I have no idea if it's true, but it's a customer service legend. Nordstrom, Inc. has long been recognized in business as an excellent, if not the premier, deliverer of quality customer service. Books and entire customer service seminars have been built around Nordstrom's customer service philosophy. The company's employee manual contains just 75 words.

In 1975 Nordstrom purchased some retail stores from the Alaska Commercial Company in Anchorage. A customer who was unaware that the store had changed hands attempted to return a set of tires purchased a few days before. Nordstrom, of course, does not and never has sold any automotive products. But the store took back the tires and cheerfully refunded the full purchase price, retaining a satisfied customer. The story was related on the front page of the *Wall Street Journal*. You can't buy that kind of publicity.

Now, I have no way of knowing if that actually happened. What makes it significant is the length Nordstrom went to in the quest for customer satisfaction. Was it a wise thing to do? What if the following day hundreds of people arrived on the doorstep returning all kinds of items they did not purchase at Nordstrom? How long would Nordstrom continue to lose money before a policy change was warranted? Let's explore this philosophy a little further.

Can I get a steak at McDonald's? Wouldn't that be good customer service? Suppose I made a wrong turn on the freeway, and ended up at McDonald's instead of the Four Seasons. If I said, "Can't you just run to the store, grab a steak, a baked potato, and some wine and cook it up for me?" it would sound ridiculous. My expectation of the level of customer service I wanted would have fallen outside the products and services McDonald's provides its customers.

The obvious point is that when I walked into that McDonald's, several things happened. My needs and desires conflicted with the profitable operation of the business. Could they have honored my request for a steak? Of course they could, but that's not the point. Is it in their best interest to violate their business philosophy to take care of me? The answer, in this particular case, is obviously no.

Every business works very hard to satisfy the customer, but sometimes the requested service is not worth preventing the loss of a customer. In my steak analogy, it was the company, not me, that dictated the level of service that would be provided.

Now, this concept may fly in the face of all the things you've been taught about customer service over the years, but this is why it's so important that you clearly define the level of customer service you intend to provide. "The customer is always right" has always been the mantra of small business. But if you live by that mantra, you just might drive yourself out of business.

Let's look at two extremes. Extreme one: Could you, if you really applied yourself, deliver service so bad that no customer would ever come through your door again? I think that answer would be yes. Extreme two: Could you deliver service so good that you could not afford to deliver it day in, day out? An example might be sending limos to transport customers to and from your business.

As you can see, your level of customer service has to be defined somewhere between the two extremes. But there are two more components we have to add to this customer service equation, in order for it to work for you.

First, we have to make a profit. The second part of the equation is that, as much as we have been taught to constantly exceed the customer's expectation, isn't there a limit to *how long* we can accomplish that? We can do it for a short time, but sooner or later we move dangerously close to extreme number two.

In spite of the hype from customer service gurus, customers really aren't looking to be wowed. How many stores have you gone back to just to see how they are going to wow you this time? If they don't wow you enough, do you stop going? Customers want consistency. They want to walk in, have a positive shopping experience, and leave satisfied. So here is the hard-and-fast rule that defines customer service for your business:

Your customer service is the most consistent service you can deliver, day in and day out, and still be profitable. Are there times when you have to go above and beyond your standard level of service to satisfy a customer? Yes, those times are going to happen. But they are the exceptions, not the rule. You can take back the tires or go get the steak if, and only if, you can do it and still be profitable, and if doing so will build, and not hurt, your business. Live by this rule, and you will have the best customer service possible.

Now that you have the answers to all the questions in this chapter, it's time to move on to Chapter 3, and find out what to do with this information and how to begin to construct your marketing plan.

CHAPTER

3

Step 2: SWOT?

C ongratulations! Now that you've finished your business resume, it's time to see what you've got to work with. As
you analyze your resume, you should notice that you have
four areas to contemplate: strengths, weaknesses, opportunities, and
threats (SWOT).

You have some control over two of these areas, and virtually no
control over the other two. Let me define each one, and then explore
how each affects your business.

Strengths

Strengths are all the things you do well in your business. Obviously,
you want to keep doing those things, and not get too comfortable
or confident that you will always do them well. The business resume
will help you become aware of the various strengths your business
has, and you will need to match those strengths to the right target
market later on in the plan. Don't take anything in your business for

granted. This is not the time to be modest about things that make your business great or set it apart from your competitors.

Weaknesses

Weaknesses are things you don't do so well. As human beings, it's natural for us to find reasons to be self-critical. However, there is a big difference between being honest about your business and being critical of yourself. We often regard any form of personal weakness as a defect in defining who we are. When you evaluate this area of the SWOT analysis, keep in mind that we are not talking about just your personal strengths and weaknesses; we are talking about how those strengths and weaknesses affect the business. The business is a totally separate entity from you, the person.

Keep this thought in mind: Weaknesses are almost always temporary. For example, you might be able to compete more favorably with your nearest competitor if you had a larger delivery truck. The fact that you don't have a large enough truck doesn't mean you are a bad person or a poor business owner. It simply means you don't have the right truck . . . yet.

Budget your finances for the truck purchase, and someday that weakness will move into the strengths column. While you are waiting for that day to arrive, continue to compete as hard as you can, and keep in mind that the sacrifice you make today will pay off tomorrow.

Don't confuse weaknesses with where you are right now. If you want to lose 30 pounds, most doctors will tell you to lose two pounds a week—anything faster might be dangerous to your health. So you modify your diet, begin an exercise program, and work toward your goal. Do the same thing here. Each day is a journey toward a better business . . . and a better life. Don't allow temporary weaknesses to prevent the strengthening of yourself and your business, each and every day.

Opportunities

Oprah Winfrey is credited with the saying, "Luck is opportunity meeting preparation." I could not agree more.

Opportunities appear unexpectedly and without warning. They usually present themselves at the least advantageous or worst possible time, and almost always require some kind of cash outlay.

Sometimes we're ready for them; most times we're not. Sometimes we don't even recognize them as opportunities until it's too late. The best advice I can give you is to take advantage of opportunities when you can do so, and don't dwell on the big one that got away. Learn from the experience and be better prepared the next time. Put aside a little cash each month so you can be "lucky" when an opportunity presents itself.

Threats

Threats are a whole different animal. Threats are anything that can permanently damage your business. Do you remember the Tylenol scare back in the 1980s? Between September 29 and October 1, 1982, seven people in Chicago died of cyanide poisoning after taking Extra Strength Tylenol.

Johnson & Johnson, the parent company of the maker of Tylenol, had a decision to make. J&J could assume that these poisonings were one random event, and leave Tylenol on the shelf. If any lawsuits should arise, the company could simply pay off the injured parties. But if it was not an isolated incident, J&J could find itself on the hook for millions of dollars in damages. Johnson & Johnson bit the bullet, and pulled all Tylenol off the shelves. Then, at J&J's request, Calle & Company came up with Gelcaps, the first tamper-proof capsules. Over time, Tylenol regained its position as the top-selling painkiller.

If not handled correctly, threats such as those experienced by Tylenol could put you out of business in a hurry, or allow you to die a long, slow, painful death as customers desert your business. Threats have to be addressed as soon as possible, and, as in the Tylenol case, you may need to pull out all the stops to survive. It's extremely important that you are prepared to mix knowledge and preparation when dealing with threats.

The Parts of SWOT

Now that that you have the definitions of SWOT, here is how to use each one in your marketing plan. Use a single piece of paper for each of the items you listed in your business resume: principals of the company, product awareness, competition, and so on.

Draw a line down the center of each page, and list strengths and opportunities on one side, and weaknesses and threats on the other. You need to go into great detail here. Using the definitions in the previous paragraphs, you must analyze each aspect of your business. This information is also critical to the success or failure of your business plan when the time comes to visit your banker.

This will help you organize each component of your business, and let you capitalize on each strength/opportunity and deal with each weakness/threat. The first part of your resume asked you to look at the people involved with the company. Are there problems? Lack of expertise? Lack of experience?

If there are problems, how can you solve them? Or are they something you must live with? Can you deal with the problem immediately, or are you going to have to wait for a solution?

Example: Under product distribution, your product may be expensive to ship. This may cause a reduction in profit. Is it a weakness? Arranging a contract with a local shipping company may be a way to make this area into a strength. Perhaps you can reduce the shipping expenses by shipping only once a week while growing your business.

What challenges are going to be short-range? Long-range? Maybe you're working out of your basement, and space is already a problem. How long will it be before you can afford commercial space? Can you trade services for commercial space? A cleaning company may clean the building in return for a space in the building.

I realize it's hard to be self-critical, but these first two steps (resume and SWOT analysis) are by far the most important ones of the entire marketing plan. The importance of being totally and completely honest when compiling this information is paramount to your success. Glossing over any part can cause your entire plan to derail down the line.

This part of the plan can also be very depressing. The more you look, the more weaknesses you find. However, that's actually a good thing; it's exactly the result you are looking for. Sooner or later, you are going to have to deal with each of the weaknesses if you want to build a successful business. Being aware of any weaknesses will force you to think about them and find solutions. It's better to deal with and eliminate them at the beginning than for any one of them to be the final nail in your business's demise.

Imagine your first day at a gym or fitness club. You don't walk in with your tail between your legs saying, "I'm so weak I'll never be strong." You walk in knowing that with hard work and time, you are going to improve those elements of your body that you are dissatisfied with. Look at your business the same way. See it in the future the way you want it to be, and move in that direction. Recognize that there is work to be done, and you are prepared to do it. Remember, this plan is a work in progress, not an end result.

In the coming months, you will refer to these first two steps over and over again as your market changes and your business becomes stronger. Keep these work sheets in a handy place. Add and amend strengths and challenges as your business grows and prospers.

CHAPTER 4

Step 3: Sales Forecasting

First Things First (How Does the Selling Process Really Work?)

Before we move into setting sales objectives, I want to spend a moment showing you how the sales process actually works. Having been in sales all my life, it still amazes me that there is no degree in sales from any university. Nothing happens in business until someone sells something, yet there are business degrees, marketing degrees, law degrees—everything but a PhD in sales. Fortune 500 companies conduct yearly bidding wars for the top marketing graduates, yet they will hire almost any warm body to do the most important job in the company: selling the product.

One of the many jobs I held during my long sales history was that of an insurance agent for one of the major life insurance companies. In order to sell insurance, there is a long training process, as well as licensing tests, before you can become an agent. You would think life insurance salespeople would be the best of all selling professions.

In 1965, over 80 percent of all life insurance was sold by fewer than 20 percent of the salespeople. In 1990, 80 percent of all life insurance was being sold by less than 15 percent of the sales force. Salespeople in general were actually getting worse instead of better.

Sales Expertise

Every sales program has the same goal: to improve the performance of salespeople. Yet to date no books, training programs, or any other efforts have shown any overall measured improvements in salespeople's competence.

This should be when you point out to me that you don't have a sales force, so all this isn't really applicable to you. Wrong! Even if you are the sole employee who delivers a product or service to anybody, you sell! And, if you plan to be successful against your competition, you had better learn how the process works, and how to make it work for you.

So, why have most salespeople gotten worse instead of better? Two possible reasons are the two sales myths that I would like to debunk right now.

Myth Number One: If You Want to Make More Sales, Make More Calls   Hustle is the name of the game, it's said; but nothing could be further from the truth. I will agree that if you make five calls per day, day in and day out, to the right target market, something is going to happen, and you will sell something. Let me show you a better way.

How to Measure Sales   Early in my selling career, I worked for a company called Victor Business Machines. At the time, it was the number-one manufacturer of adding machines and calculators in the country. It had a very simple sales philosophy: Every Monday, make

75 cold calls to businesses, door to door. That's a great way to start your week, huh? If you have a problem with rejection, it's probably not the job for you.

My objective, out of the 75 cold calls, was to find 20 businesses that would allow me to place one of our many products in their business to try for a couple of days. Of the 20 products placed, the national sales average at that time was five sales. Seventy-five cold calls netted 20 placements, which then equaled five sales.

If I'm working this system, what are my objectives? Do I want to make 75 cold calls to get those 20 placements? No! My goal is to make the 20 placements with as few cold calls as possible. That's where the real secret of selling comes in—measurement.

Each Monday, I would measure how many cold calls it took to make the 20 placements. If I got a "no," before I made the next call I would review in my mind what happened with that call. What could I have done differently? How could I have overcome that objection? Was that business a valid customer for my products?

I had to constantly improve my ability to find or develop a need in the customer's mind for my products. Over time I discovered that I was going to hear only about a half dozen valid objections. As I learned to overcome those, my placement rate improved, and I had to make fewer cold calls.

Next, I was expected to make five sales out of the 20 placements. At first I was inexperienced, and I wasn't doing that. Once again, I had to measure what was going on with each demonstration and close. As I improved at presentation, overcoming objections, and demonstrating value, my closing ratio also improved. So, what was my objective here? To make five sales, or to make *more than* five sales? Very good—more than five sales was precisely what I wanted to do.

So, was I making more calls, or was I working smarter? Go to the head of the class. Yes, I was working smarter. Only two things will improve selling performance: an increase in the salesperson's knowledge and information (product knowledge) and more disciplined selling skills (measuring what is going on with each sale, and learning from each contact).

Myth Number Two: Salespeople Work to Meet Sales Quotas   You may think salespeople work for you to meet company goals, and monetary incentives will improve performance. Wrong! There isn't a salesperson alive who works primarily to achieve the sales quotas of any company.

Salespeople work toward their personal, individual monetary goals for themselves and their families (sending kids to college, paying the mortgage, etc.). If the benefits to the company conflict with the benefits to the employee, which do you think will be more important to the employee—the company or the employee's family?

Find Their Real Motivation   If you want to motivate a salesperson positively, find out what he or she is interested in. What is the salesperson's one overpowering burning desire? It may not be money. Some people just want to be appreciated for their efforts. What about the clerk in the retail store? What is more money per hour worth if you have to go to a job where the boss ignores your efforts? Most people, if given the choice, will give up cash in exchange for appreciation for their performance. Hundreds of studies support this position. Read *In Search of Excellence*, by Tom Peters and Robert Waterman (Harper & Row, 1982).

Get Personal   Get to know your employees on a personal level. Support them and help them achieve their goals, and they will move mountains. Encourage them to measure their efforts, and teach them how to improve performance as a way of reaching their personal goals. You'll keep good employees, and you'll develop a sales force to be reckoned with—even if your sales force is only you.

One-Inch Drill Bit?

Why would I ever buy a one-inch drill bit? So I can display it over the fireplace for all my guests to see? No, I buy a one-inch drill bit because I want a one-inch hole. I don't want the drill bit itself; I want the benefit of the drill bit—the hole! I want the benefit of the product. I don't buy a copier; I buy 1,000,000 copies over a seven-year period. This is how you need to see your product or service before you present it to your customers.

Seven Selling Steps

Let's look at the seven selling steps and how they work.

Step 1: Greeting and Acknowledging the Customer

Your customers can purchase from either you or your competitor, and how you interact with them can have a strong impact on their decision. If you took a survey comparing the friendliness of people in small towns versus big cities, small towns would probably win hands down.

It's a national perception that people in small towns are generally friendlier and go out of their way for folks. People in New York City, by contrast, are perceived as rude, and for some reason seem to be proud of it. Courtesy is a skill you can perfect into a productive habit. Courteous people have practiced being courteous, have perfected that skill into a productive habit, and are not even aware they are being courteous.

In contrast, aggressive and pushy people have formed those habits, and are not aware they are aggressive and pushy. It is physically and emotionally impossible to be polite and courteous, as well as aggressive and pushy, at the same time. You can't be polite and courteous at work, and not at home. Either it is a habit you have perfected or it isn't. Start being as polite and courteous as you can be, all day, every day, for the next 21 days. Research says if you do something at the same time, in the same way, for 21 consecutive days, it becomes a habit.

How's Your Climate?   How is the climate in your town? No, not the weather climate—the friendliness climate. What is the friendliness level of people where you live—polite and courteous, or aggressive and pushy? For example, in Bozeman, Montana, on a scale of 1 to 10, with 10 being so friendly strangers would lend you their cars, Bozeman is probably a 6.

The population here turns over about every 7 to 10 years (mostly due to the weather). Every six or seven years, a few days at minus 30 degrees will convince some folks that Arizona might be better. We get a lot of transplants escaping the big city for the friendlier small town. They sometimes bring the aggressive and pushy attitude they learned in their former home to their new home.

Local businesspeople want to maintain a friendliness standard of 7 or above. If they can do that, they know the majority of customers will take notice, and the business owners hope the customers will remember how well they were treated, compared to other businesses.

In a city, because of the large customer base, a company can lose a few customers and still do well. In a small town, with everybody knowing everybody else, it's much more important to acquire, and keep, customers. If you are an employee of a company, show the next few sentences to your company owner, boss, or supervisor.

Be a Good Listener   Listen up, business owners: Customer service starts at the top. It doesn't start at the counter or the sales floor. It starts with you. How do you treat your employees? I promise you this: Your employees will treat customers in the exact way they are treated by you. If you constantly find fault with them, that attitude will be passed on to the customer. If they are proud of their position and performance in your company, and are appreciated and encouraged by management, that is also passed on to the customer. The better they feel about themselves, the better they will treat your customers.

Have you ever eaten in a McDonald's restaurant? For this example, let's suppose you're on vacation somewhere you've never been before, and you spot a McDonald's. How confident are you that if you go inside, it's going to be pretty much the same as your hometown McDonald's? You can be highly confident, because all McDonald's restaurants operate from the same manual on how they should look, sound, and cook.

We expect a certain level of service from some businesses. We always expect our bankers to be in white shirts and ties. We don't expect the same from our auto mechanics. What should your customers expect from your business?

Question: If your very best friend walked in the front door of your business, how would you treat him or her? Treat everyone that way, because you can bet your competition doesn't.

Last, but certainly not least, get the person's name, if you don't know it, and use it frequently during the initial interview. Most people aren't extended the courtesy of hearing their name at a business. Make yours the exception. As Dale Carnegie said, "A person's name is, to that person, the sweetest and most important sound, in any language." If you don't believe that, try calling someone Bob whose name is actually Steve, and see how quickly you're corrected.

Step 2: Discovering Customer Needs

How much can I stress the importance of this portion of the selling process? If you don't have what the customer needs, you are wasting your time, and theirs, to continue with the process. If you don't discover customer needs immediately, it is costing you money in the selling process.

Here's how:

I sold furniture for eight years. Early in my sales career, I was taught many valuable lessons about the sales process by professionals in the business. For example, when a customer asked to see a dinette set, nine out of 10 salespeople would escort them to the area of the store where all the dinette sets were, and start showing them to the customer. If a sale was eventually made, it had been a time-consuming exercise of elimination of all dinette sets except one.

Time is money in retail. You have only so many hours to meet your monthly sales quota. The correct, and much faster, way to make this sale is to first discover the customer's needs by asking questions. The kinds of questions you want to ask are called open-ended questions.

Open-ended questions can't be answered by a simple yes or no. They require the customer to provide information. "What kind of dinette set do you have now? What do you like about it? What don't you like about it? What about size? Shape? Color? Natural wood grain? Formica top? Vinyl seats? Fabric? Price range?"

As I collect the information, I am adding and deleting merchandise in my mind that will or will not fit the description of what the customer is telling me. Once I have that information, I can then say to the customer, "Based on what you've told me, I have three dinette sets that will meet your needs. If you'll come this way, we'll take a look at them."

Using this method, what have I told the customer? "I'm not here as a store tour guide. I'm interested in you, and I'm taking my time to find the right dinette set for you. I don't want to waste your time, and mine, showing you things that don't fit your needs. I'm not here to sell you; I'm here to help you buy."

Step 3: Selling Merchandise Benefits

Remember our drill bit. I don't want the product; I want the benefit of the product. Recall our dinette set. Before the customer looks at any products, I ask several questions and decide on a choice for that customer, who is thinking, "At last, maybe this salesperson has what I want and I can stop shopping."

Now, as I demonstrate the product, I point out how the product fills each need within the price range the customer said he or she wanted to spend. If I go to a product that is higher in price than the customer wanted to spend, then I need to justify the extra expense with some form of benefit that is of value to that customer.

Step 4: Addressing Concerns (More Commonly Known as Overcoming Objections)

Let's go back to measuring for a moment. Remember, I mentioned the importance of measuring what happens each and every time you make or lose a sale. If you are getting a lot of objections, you are not doing a good job in the second step, discovering customer needs.

There are two kinds of objections: valid and invalid.

No salesperson should make an effort to overcome a valid objection. A valid objection means the person does not have any need for the benefits of what is being sold, or that the cost cannot be made to fit within his or her budget. This person is not a valid customer.

An invalid objection, on the other hand, is almost always a request for more information.

"Well, it looks good, but I need to think about it before I spend that much." Translation: "You haven't shown me enough benefits to justify the price."

Objections should be welcomed. They are buying signals. "Help me buy your product" is what the customer is really saying. "You haven't shown me the value yet." Don't ever show or talk about a feature unless you have a real benefit for the customer.

There's an old adage among attorneys: Never ask a witness a question you don't already know the answer to. It's the same with customers. If you don't know something, admit it, and get the answer for them as soon as possible.

Step 5: Suggesting Additional Merchandise

Most people, at this point, would probably go straight for the close, and that's fine. A sale is a sale. But this is an ideal time to suggest additional things that will enhance the sale for the customer. You can also use additional merchandise as a closing question. I'll tie the two together in the sixth step, closing the sale.

What additional types of merchandise can you sell your customer? One of the most common in appliance sales is the dreaded "extended service agreement." That's extra coverage to make sure the product performs as it's supposed to after the product warranty expires. When I worked at Circuit City, the national appliance retail giant, a percentage of my total sales had to consist of service contracts. The interesting thing about service contracts is that some people always buy them and some people never buy them, and everyone else falls somewhere in between.

I didn't try to sell a service contract at the end of the sale as if it was an add-on to the sale. I planted seeds during the sales presentation about quality and about how our service would preserve that quality, and it almost became an assumption that the customer would want the service contract.

In the car business, it's undercoating. In women's clothing, it's a matching handbag, belt, shoes, and so on. Add-on selling is certainly nothing new, and can be almost automatic, if done correctly. It is also commonly referred to as "suggestive" selling.

Keep in mind that in suggestive selling, just as in the other steps, there must be a value or benefit to the customer to any add-on. Also keep in mind that we never want to cheat, manipulate, mislead, or pressure customers to purchase anything they don't want. If the value and the need are there, why would the customer not purchase? No high pressure should be necessary.

Step 6: Closing the Sale (Asking for the Order)

Now is the time to close the sale. This is the most difficult function of the selling process for the inexperienced salesperson, and probably the easiest for the professional. The overwhelming reason most people give for not buying a product? "No one asked me to. No one asked me to buy the product." I almost fell over the first time I read that. Shouldn't that be a no-brainer?

Shouldn't we be asking customers to buy our products? Fear of rejection is pretty powerful. We will risk losing the sale before we'll face the disgrace of rejection by the customer. Most salespeople wait for the customer to buy, and if that doesn't happen, they blame the loss of the sale on price, delivery options, or any other excuse they can think of, except the real one: They simply did not ask for the order. Even the best salespeople in the world don't sell every customer they meet. But the best salespeople will always ask for the order.

How to Close   Let's explore how to ask for the order. The first step in the closing process is to become familiar with what is called the "trial close." Trial closes are nonthreatening questions you can ask the prospect that indicate where you are in the sale process. As a rule of thumb, I usually asked three trial closing questions, just to make sure I was on the same page as the customer.

An example of a trial close question might be: "Would this color work in the room?" "Are you thinking of trading in your present car?" "How soon will you need this installed?" If this color won't work, then asking for the order is useless. This is the true value of the trial close process. If you and the customer are not communicating, you need to return to the second step, discovering customer needs, to get better color information, then reevaluate your product choices for this customer and restart the process.

However, if the customer exclaims with great enthusiasm, "This color would be perfect!" that's a pretty strong buying signal. You may want to go straight to the close here, or if you still think there are questions, ask another trial close question. If you get yet another positive response, the customer is probably waiting for you to take control of the sale and ask for the order.

My wife will tell you that I hate to spend money on stuff, even if I know we need it. I will buy clothing for her all day long and never think a thing about it. But buying a shirt or tie for myself is another story. I always justify the position that I can always get by a little longer with what I've got.

My point is, I'm the type of person who wants to buy, but if you don't ask me, you'll lose the sale. What can you do that will move me off the fence and get me to say yes?

Here are the more popular techniques for closing the sale.

Assumed Close or Order Blank Close　In this close, you simply assume that you have a sale, and begin to fill out the sales order.

"What is the delivery address?"

If the customer gives you the address without objection, he or she has bought the merchandise.

Major/Minor Close　In this close, the customer makes a major purchase by answering a minor question.

"Would you prefer delivery on Tuesday or Thursday?"

"Thursday would be better for us."

You just made the sale.

"Answer the Objection" Close　In this close, you answer the customer's objection and then go to either the assumed close or the major/minor close.

"We can't be home during the week for delivery."

"We deliver on Saturday. Would morning or afternoon be better for you?"

"Morning would be better."

Done deal.

"Third Person" Close This is a very strong close. If a satisfied customer referred the current customer to your business, you can relate how happy the friend is with the product, the service, and the delivery, and it's a natural progression that the current customer wants the same level of satisfaction.

"Ben Franklin" Close In this close the salesperson uses a sheet of paper and draws a line down the center. On the left are the negatives of the product, and on the right are the positives and the reasons the customer should buy.

Take notes during the questioning phase of the second step, discovering customer needs; then list the very items the customer asked for on the right. The customer can quickly see that the advantages of having the product far outweigh the disadvantages of not buying.

"Yes Momentum" Close Picture a huge boulder rolling down a hillside. At first it starts rolling slowly; then it gradually picks up speed until it's rolling at breakneck speed. The increased speed is momentum.

With our customer, we don't want to increase the speed of our speech, but we do want to create a momentum of the customer saying yes, yes, yes, to a series of questions. We are looking for agreement from the customer that the benefits of the product will fill the customer's needs, and the momentum confirms that.

"What Does It Cost?" Close In the case of an automobile, a refrigerator, or a copier machine, there are costs that are required to keep the product in operation. An automobile customer may be looking for the best gas mileage. What is the monthly cost of electricity to operate a refrigerator? Can your model cut costs? A laser printer will need toner cartridges, and the cost per copy may be cheaper for the customer with your model.

We all want to save money as long as we don't have to sacrifice the benefits of the product. So, show value, and you will have a sale.

"Bonus" Close   Some customers just like to get a little something extra. Some type of bonus, such as free delivery, extra service, or some other incentive, may make the difference for these customers.

You don't want to give the store away in this type of close. It should be a confirmation of the order, not "one from column A and one from column B." "If I add free delivery, do we have a deal?" If not, then free delivery comes off the bargaining table.

"What Will It Take to Get Your Business?" Close   "Mr. Customer, I know this product will do the job for you." "I know you'll like it." Ask, "What do we have to do to get your business?" Then shut up and listen. In many cases, it might be some minor concern that you can easily take care of.

Another advantage is that it lets the customer have some limited control of the sale. It also shows that you are willing to work with the customer, and gives you added credibility in the customer's eyes.

"Reduction to Ridiculous" Close   If your customer is anything like me, you need to show me that my objections are just a smoke screen. I want the product, but I just don't want to say yes for some reason. Don't insult your customer by saying his or her objections are ridiculous. You can show that in an implied manner by detailing each objection and overcoming it.

You hope they will see how silly they are being and make the purchase. In the long run, this is what you're always trying to do with customers: show them the disadvantages of not buying.

Step 7: Assuring Satisfaction

Ever have buyer's remorse—that sickening feeling in the pit of your stomach that you might have made a mistake in your purchase? You paid too much? You should have gotten the other one you looked at? Sometimes buyers need you to reinforce to them that they made the correct decision. Otherwise, you may see them again in a few days—in the return line.

Operating a business in a small town demands that every customer must be a satisfied customer. There is a two-edged sword called "word of mouth" that can make or break a small town business. Positive word of mouth can be the best possible advertising you can get. If you react too slowly to customer dissatisfaction, negative word of mouth can put you out of business, quickly and permanently.

Follow-up on every sale is crucial. Make sure the customer is absolutely satisfied with your business in every way. Make it easy for your customers to complain about anything they're unhappy with. Most of us want to avoid complaints and confrontation with angry customers, and we take on the "They aren't going to get the best of me" attitude.

There always seems to be the fear that unhappy customers will demand free products or services from you for life. You must face these folks and resolve their problems, while showing them you are a fair and honest business they can have confidence in. These problems must be addressed as quickly as possible. If you ignore them, they will fester and escalate into negative publicity or possible lawsuits.

However, customers rarely want to rip anyone off. If they feel they have been wronged, all they usually want is to be heard. They seldom have unreasonable demands.

Ask them to explain exactly what the problem is, then shut up and listen. Don't interrupt to make your points until they have finished. Restate their complaint back to them so they are sure you understand and have heard what they are saying. Then simply ask, "What would you like us to do to resolve your problem?"

If you listen and refrain from arguing, you will find in many cases that they will apologize to you for flying off the handle and thank you for resolving the problem . . . and you have retained a customer.

Nothing is more valuable than a satisfied customer, who will help your business like nothing else can by relating a positive experience to other potential customers. Can you use them in your ads or commercials? Testimonials in small towns are very powerful. The more respected the person, the more powerful the testimonial.

Now that we know the basics of selling, let's get back to sales forecasting.

Sales Forecasting Principles and Tools

In order to do a good job of forecasting sales, you will need to have some goals and objectives you want your sales forecasting to achieve.

What are sales objectives? In a nutshell, they are the amount of business that must be done to keep the doors of your business open. If you don't generate enough sales, you are out of business. According to your business resume that you did at the start of this plan, you say you can do certain things and have certain abilities. The next step is to translate these things and abilities into sales.

Determining Sales Objectives

How do we determine our sales objectives? I like to start at the end and work backwards.

Remember the Victor Business Machines story I told you earlier in the book? Seventy-five cold calls for 20 placements equals five sales. Our sales objectives must be based on the end result of what we expect our business to accomplish monetarily.

Our objectives must be challenging, yet attainable. The market must be of sufficient size to support the business (remember the six gas stations). All marketing programs are based in real time. We must set time-specific goals for our sales objectives to be completed. We need both short-term objectives (one year) and long-term objectives (three to five years). We must also consider projected profits. We must make sufficient plans to realize enough income to pay the bills and, we hope, pay ourselves.

Now, if you've been in business for a number of years, you can use past performance as an indication of how your business is growing, or not growing, as the case may be. Speaking of growing, I can't tell you how many business owners have told me, "I really don't want to get any bigger." I'll let you in on a little secret: You don't have a choice. I know you think you do, but, believe me, you don't. Your business will eventually take on a life of its own, and it will do the dictating to you as to what you will or won't do. You will do it or you will be out of business.

Make some projections for the future.

If this is your first business, you are going to have to make some educated guesses and get some outside help. One place to start is the public library. You can start with *Ulrich's Periodicals Directory*, published annually by R. R. Bowker. I don't care what kind of business you're in; there is a trade magazine or newsletter that covers it. Magazines survey their subscribers about a host of topics. How do you advertise? What's your advertising budget? How do you promote your business? What are your business projections for the next five years?

Subscribe to as many trade magazines as possible. Some of them can be expensive. Write each one and tell them you are in the business and ask them for the qualifications of a free subscription. In my field, I have free subscriptions to *Target Marketing*, *Direct Marketing News*, *Business Marketing*, *NetWeek*, and *Publish*, just to name a few. It's in their best interest to provide free subscriptions to serious people in the business, because those are the exact people the advertisers are trying to reach.

Another good resource for the new business owner is the *Small Business Sourcebook*, published annually by Gale Research. Your library should have a copy. If not, it can surely borrow it from another branch. This book has ratios, budgets, and other helpful information about a large variety of businesses.

Next, the library also has *The Encyclopedia of Associations* (Thomson Gale, published annually). Again, almost any industry you can name has some kind of association. And what's the purpose of an association? To work for the success of the members of the association, of course. These people are also at your disposal to assist you with market research regarding your industry. You can also meet successful people in your industry who are more than willing to help you (unless they are direct competitors of yours). Look for another town like your hometown (preferably in another state, because a similar business in the next town is probably your competitor).

For Bozeman, Montana, I use Boulder, Colorado, for business information. It's approximately the same size as Bozeman, a college town, and has similar distances to other cities and comparable housing costs, taxes, and forms of government.

If you were going to open a bakery, for example, you would get on the phone and call some bakeries in Boulder. Ask if they would share where the industry is going in the next one to three years. Some will talk with you, and some won't. Talk to the ones who will. Save their time, and yours, by making a list of the topics you want to talk to them about, and go down the list. The conversation will go faster, and the person called will appreciate your consideration of their time.

Business Costs

Next, you are going to have monthly fixed and variable costs of operation. Fixed costs remain the same regardless of whether a single sale is made. Variable costs increase or decrease based on the number of sales made. Fixed costs are things like the rent or equipment leases.

Variable costs might be monthly shipping charges, cost of supplies, sales commissions—any expense that changes from month to month. If you aren't sure which they are, consider them fixed. Other things to consider would be things like insurance, maintenance, payroll, utilities, automobile, and advertising costs, to name just a few.

Break-Even Analysis

When you have your costs under control, you need to consider a break-even analysis for each product or service you provide. The break-even analysis assumes that average variable costs are going to remain constant for each product or service. This analysis is strictly internal. It doesn't consider things like competition or market demand.

What's the formula?

Are you sure you're ready for this? Okay, stay with me here. Total profit equals the number of units sold, multiplied by the selling price less the number of units sold, multiplied by the total variable cost, minus the total fixed cost. Pretty simple, huh?

If P is profit, U is units sold, p is price, V is variable costs, and F is fixed costs, the equation would look like this:

$$P = U(p - V) - F$$

So, assume your bakery produces cakes and you want to sell 1,000 of them for $10 each. For this example, your total fixed costs are going to be $7,700 and your total variable costs are $4.50 per unit. (These numbers are for demonstration use only and may not accurately reflect bakery industry norms.)

Your formula would look like this:

$$P = 1,000(\$10 - \$4.50) - \$7,700$$
$$= \$5,500 - \$7,700$$
$$= -\$2,200$$

What happened?

Instead of making money, you just lost $2,200. If you were breaking even, the $2,200 number should be $0. You will lose money on 1,000 units with current costs and pricing, so how many cakes must you really sell to break even?

Since your fixed costs (F) are still $7,700, the selling price (p) is still $10, and your variable costs (V) are still $4.50 per unit, you do this:

Take (p) price minus (V) variable costs, and divide the difference into (F) fixed costs:

$$\$10 - \$4.50 = \$5.50$$

$$\$7,700 \div \$5.50 = 1,400 \, \text{cakes}$$

If you maintain your current pricing and expenses, you need to sell 1,400 cakes to break even. If you either raise your price or reduce your expenses, you can sell less and still break even.

Some points to remember: The break-even analysis is always going to be a work in progress. Perhaps cakes make a profit, but cupcakes don't. Even though a product breaks even (or makes a profit), if all other goods and services don't, you could be in trouble.

Business owners often tend to look only at the bottom line. There are many cases where a break-even analysis can help spotlight the aspects of your business that might be costing rather than making you money. Even a car in need of a tune-up will get you to work, but it burns more gas than it should. The entire company may be making a profit, which is a good thing, but the company would be stronger if all cylinders were firing.

This is a guide to get you started. The break-even analysis I'm using here may not be the ideal one for you. Do an Internet search for "break-even analysis" and find one that works for you. My formula is a very simple one, designed to show the principle of how the break-even analysis works. Many industry associations have formulas available to their members that might be a better fit for your business.

Good accountants are worth their weight in gold. Take this basic information and have them tailor it to your business. Have them explain how to record all the business transactions you do during your workday. For example, does your business card printing go under office expense or advertising? Having all your ducks in the right rows will also make your life a lot easier in case the Internal Revenue Service (IRS) decides to audit your tax returns.

Once you have compiled the information showing how much it will cost to keep the doors open and the business viable, we can move on to the next part of the marketing plan.

Step 4: Who and Where Are Your Customers?

Finding the Target

I n this part of the plan I will show you how to identify your target market. How do you find a needle in a haystack? The most difficult and time-consuming way is to remove each piece of hay until only the needle is left. And, in the long run, that would certainly work. But the easiest way is to use a very powerful magnet.

Business works the same way. The needle, and only the needle, is attracted to the magnet. So target marketing involves identifying the needles (your ideal customers), and then creating the right type of magnet (advertising message) that will attract enough of them to keep you in business.

Let's start by thinking about what we already know. If you've been in business for a time, you might already have a picture in your mind of your ideal customers. What do you know about them? How did they find you? Why do they deal with you, rather than a competitor? How can you reach more people like them? Next, let's look at the market as a whole.

Who are the people most likely to use your product or service? The smaller the town, the easier it is to answer this question. If you live in a town of 1,000 or fewer people, its demographics may have similar percentages of age, education, and home ownership as large cities, but the numbers represented by those percentages are in double digits, not based on a 100,000 population.

If you live in a town of 1,000 people, 750 of whom are over the age of 70 and on fixed incomes, and you're selling life insurance, you may be in trouble. They may want to buy, but can they afford it? Can you sell enough to the other 250 to make a living?

Demographics of your sales region are very important to your business health. There must be enough potential customers in your town or county, of the right age, income level, education, and so on, to support your business. I worked with a company in San Diego that wanted to erect a sports complex where Major League Baseball players could conduct clinics for kids during the off-season.

The *San Diego Union* newspaper had conducted a demographic study of the entire county. Using that study, I was able to pinpoint the zip codes that had the largest populations of kids 8 to 13 years of age. Advertising targeted to those zip codes, and those parents, produced more customers than we could imagine. Several clinics had to be added.

Can you sell to the world? We have many businesses in Montana that don't make a dime selling to anyone in their hometowns or even in Montana. The majority of their business is done out of state and/or out of the country. They just enjoy living here. If you live in or have visited San Diego, California, you may have gone to see a ball game at Qualcomm Stadium. Qualcomm has an office in Bozeman.

Ross Perot's old company, Electronic Data Systems Corporation (EDS), has an office here. Gibson Guitar Corporation makes some of the finest guitars in the world here. If you qualified for an American Express card, there is a good chance that your approval was done by Zoot Industries in Bozeman.

As you can see, it doesn't really matter where your target market is, as long as you know *who* they are, and have the ability and resources to reach them. That's what it's really all about. Who are these people? Very simply, they are a group of people with common characteristics, who behave in a predictable manner.

The first step in target marketing is to determine whether your primary target group will include purchasers, users, or both. Which group has the most need for the product? Who actually buys the product, and how do they select what they buy?

Second, does your target group's demographics coincide with your present customers? This is particularly tough in bigger cities. An area of a few blocks may be a who's who of ethnic groups, all with different emotional buying buttons. In the flyover states, there is usually one large ethnic group, with a few smaller groups mixed in. Demographics play a large role in determining who your target market really is.

Third, how do your customers buy the products and services they use? Who buys and who uses? These might be two entirely different groups.

Is 67 percent of your business done by 33 percent of your total customers? If so, then the 67 percent users become your primary target market. The 33 percent is your secondary market. For example: 67 percent of the beer drinkers are men, but only 33 percent actually go to the store and buy it themselves. For the majority, their wives do the shopping and purchasing. The men would appear to be the secondary market from a purchasing standpoint, but they are actually the primary market as the end users of the product.

Now, here is the real challenge in target marketing. Staying with our beer analogy, do we target the men who are the drinkers, or do we concentrate our efforts on appealing to the women who actually make the purchase? Confusing? That's what makes target marketing so much fun. As you can see, guessing at who your market really is can cost you big bucks if you advertise to the wrong group with the wrong message. Take the time to thoroughly analyze all your target markets.

Can You Be All Things to All People?

Let's look at one of my favorite companies: McDonald's. McDonald's has spent billions of dollars on advertising, becoming *the* family restaurant. The restaurants have the kids' Happy Meal, offer the Big Mac for Mom and Dad, and give away every toy on the planet that's tied to any current action-adventure movie. So, the question becomes: Can McDonald's attract a new market that is diametrically opposed to the one it has spent so much money and effort cultivating?

Have you bought an Arch Deluxe lately? What's an Arch Deluxe, you ask? How quickly we forget. It was introduced in 1996 as the flagship adult sandwich of McDonald's, and was one of biggest fast-food flops of all time. McDonald's thought they could capture more of the adult market being taken by Wendy's at the time. (Remember "Where's the beef?")

Not only was the Arch Deluxe a health nightmare of high calories and fat, but the advertising over time began to erode the other McDonald's brands. The campaign was eventually shelved after a total cost of over $100 million.

When I see a playground out front, do I think I'm going into an adult restaurant? The Arch Deluxe, the MacLean burger, and other adult fare died slow and horrible deaths. You would think McDonald's would have learned from its "light and healthy" salad menu a few years before, which was also a failure.

People who eat healthy wouldn't choose McDonald's. It is going after a target market that past experience says is the wrong market. What's next, the Diabetic Deluxe? When you're a company the size of McDonald's, it's possible to survive a $100 million hit, painful as it was. The smaller business owner doesn't have that luxury. It doesn't matter if you're big or small, the wrong market is the wrong market; but in a small town the wrong market will end your business.

Do It Right

Let me show you the right way to do this. Here are 10 guidelines:

1. *Look at your total market.* Continually identify all types and categories of people, industries, and others that might use your product or service. If I open a store selling baby products, how many markets will I have? I will have new moms, their co-workers and friends for the baby shower, their brothers and sisters, and their grandmas and grandpas, to name just a few.

2. *Break it down.* Break down your list of potential markets into groups that have common characteristics. For example, list people by professions or industries. If you were selling photocopiers, what groups would you look for? One common trait would be paper use. Attorneys use tons of paper. How about real estate agents or insurance agents? A bakery or clothing store might not use nearly as much.

3. *Analyze your markets.* Discover as much as possible about the groups you have segmented. What do they like? Not like? What do they want? What do they fear? Who do they buy from now? Why do they buy from them? How much sales potential does this target group have? How can you sell them?

4. *Study the competition.* How do your competitors do it? What are they doing that is working in your market? Can you do something similar? Can you acquire some of their market share?

5. *Prioritize.* Rank market segments by priority. Your primary market should be the easiest to reach with the lowest investment and greatest expectation of return. Don't forget to do your break-even analysis of each market. The market may be great, but if it's not a profitable market, then it's a waste of time and money to pursue it.

6. *Do an in-depth market analysis of your top markets.* Uncover as much information as you can about your most likely customers, including what they read, what trends they are concerned about, and how they think. Who do they consider best in your field and why?

7. *What forms of marketing are most successful?* We are all bombarded by thousands of advertising messages every day. It's no wonder advertising is such a science. How do you fight all those competitive messages and still get customers to even hear, let alone pay attention to, your messages?

   Studies show that if people hear about your business or service four or more times, they perceive you as credible. The fewer resources a company wastes (marketing to people who will never be prospects), the more it can invest reaching and selling to its genuine prospects. Asking "How did you hear about us?" can help zero in on ways to reach new customers. Be consistent in your marketing. You need to be in front of your market as often as your budget allows. Slow and steady wins the race. One-time or flash-in-the-pan advertising is usually a waste of money.

8. *Test your markets.* At a marketing seminar in San Diego, California, that I attended, one of the companies presenting was King Schools. King Schools sells a video course that assists pilots in passing their pilot's license exam. The company priced the course at around $250 because that price beat out $199 and $159 in a test of three different markets. Prospects who received

information about the $159 and $199 course thought it was too good to be true at those low prices and didn't buy.

9. *What do you have to do?* How many customers must walk through your door, or how many sales calls must be made, before a sale takes place? Once again, the secret of selling customers is measurement. Start each salesperson out each day with 50 business cards. Each prospect they talk to gets a card, whether the prospect buys or not. At the end of the day, count the sales and the cards. This will give you a good idea of the salesperson's closing ratio. If the salesperson has 10 cards left and made five sales, it means that 35 people walked out the door without buying. These numbers might be good or bad, depending on the type of product you sell. If it's farm machinery at $250,000 each, that might be a great closing ratio. The point is, once the salesperson knows that 35 people are walking, he or she can work on making that number 34.

10. *Choose your markets carefully.* Keep in mind that it's not how many target markets you can identify and open; it's how many you can profitably penetrate, market to, and serve. There's nothing wrong with opening as many as possible, as long as they make money and you have the resources and personnel to handle them all. Treat your target market as an open-ended question, always changing and providing new information.

Finding your most profitable target markets is a top priority. If you aren't selling to the right people, you won't have a business for long. The smaller the town, the smaller the total customer base, and the quicker the death of your business.

CHAPTER 6

Step 5: How to Create Your Plan and Make It Work

Now that you know your target market, the next step is to develop the marketing objectives and marketing strategies to reach those customers. Let's start by defining the two terms.

Marketing Objective

A marketing objective is the end result of what needs to be accomplished. You might assign different marketing objectives to different parts of your business. A florist might want to expand into landscaping. Each activity would have its own marketing strategies and objectives.

Your marketing objectives must be specific. Each must focus on one singular goal. They must also be measurable. There must be a specific time period for a clear demonstration of success: one month?

six months? two years? Whatever the time, it must be specific. There also needs to be a method of accountability by someone at the end of the time period.

Objectives can also relate to specific parts of the marketing plan. A company might have an overall objective, and various divisions within the company might have their own objectives, which would be part of the total company's marketing objective.

Marketing Strategy

A marketing strategy details the steps of how each individual marketing objective will be achieved. It describes the method of accomplishment. Like our marketing objectives, our marketing strategies must also be clearly defined, and tell exactly how the objectives will be met. A game of Monopoly isn't much fun if you don't read the rules first. There is an object to the game, which is why we play it.

Another example might be a football game. The objective is to win the game. The strategies are the plays used to accomplish this. The objective has a specific time period assigned to it: the length of the game. It focuses on one specific goal: winning the game. The strategies, in contrast, change as the game goes on, due to injuries, weather, the score of the game, field position, the play clock, and strengths and weaknesses of the opposing team. There are four measurements during the game that enable us to determine how successful we are, called quarters. Even if we are behind in the first three quarters, if we are ahead at the end of the fourth quarter our objective has been successfully met.

Suppose you have a baby products store, and your sales objective is to increase sales 10 percent over the previous quarter. You have a specific and measurable goal: 10 percent sales increase over a three-month period.

Some of the strategies you might use to accomplish your goal are:

Your primary target markets are pregnant women and new mothers with infants up to three years of age. One possible secondary target market is new grandparents.

You'll want to focus your advertising efforts on reaching these two groups. You need to know, from your target market research, what newspapers they read, television shows they watch, radio stations they listen to, and so on. Also keep in mind that you can't ignore your existing customers. You must keep their loyalty. Don't try to change your business as McDonald's tried to do, but modify it without changing the perception that you've already developed in the minds of your current customers.

Put your marketing department, which may consist of only you, to work on a marketing plan to reach the target markets. Perhaps a mailing to all new mothers in the area would be a good starting point. How do you find them? By checking birth records at the county courthouse.

Plan a big sale for the month in which most babies are born. If you didn't know, it's September. My personal theory is that September is nine months after Christmas and New Year's Eve, when we all seem to love each other the most.

You could package a ready-made baby shower plan, with everything needed to put on a successful baby shower. This could be as simple as a "top 20" list you type up on your letterhead and send out to people who request it. But how will your customers know you even have it? Your advertising would say, "Send for our 'Top Twenty Tips for Planning a Successful Baby Shower.'" More people might consider giving a baby shower if there was some indication they would be successful.

Next, can you lure any customers away from your competitors? Can you develop new customers who have never purchased baby products before? As you can see, the 10 percent objective can come from a wide variety of sales strategies.

In order for this section of the marketing plan to be successful, you must have very specific objectives. There must not be any gray areas. The more exact and specific you can be about your objectives, the greater probability your strategies will be successful.

Some areas of strategies might be regional, competitive, pricing, and publicity strategies.

Regional Strategy

George H.W. Bush visited Montana during his reelection campaign in 1992. The only problem was that his aides didn't do their homework and scheduled his visit on the first day of deer hunting season. George Bush or a 10-point buck? A lot of folks missed seeing George that day. Is your business region specific? Does it have any other specific conditions? No one makes sales calls to accountants in March or April. After April 15th might be okay.

Competitive Strategy

What can you do about the competition? Examine the SWOT of your business resume: Do you have an opportunity or a challenge? If your competition has the advantage, move on to another area. Don't dwell on the things you can't do anything about. But if there is an area you can exploit, then try to work it into a strategy. Unless your competitors have 100 percent of the market, you still have other strategies.

Pricing Strategy

It's not a good idea to invite your customers to examine your products strictly on price. A price-only strategy eliminates value, and that's what you are really selling. The lower the price, the lower the perceived value of the product in the customer's mind. Can you be priced lower than the competition? Sure. How hard is it to lower your price? You may find yourself having to defend your lower price, much like your higher-priced competitor must justify its higher one.

Wal-Mart has been very successful in the low-price arena, but mostly on its store brands and some specials. For example, the price of Tide is very close to supermarket pricing in Wal-Mart, as are other name brands.

Most major brands set the lowest allowed selling price for their products. If you attempt to sell them below that, there is a good possibility the company will pull the line from your store. In some cases, you will see an ad saying, "We can't mention the brand name at this low price." Sometimes companies do make exceptions, but usually only on a very short-term, strictly controlled basis.

Publicity Strategy

Do you know how most people or businesses get mentioned in the newspaper? In the mid-1980s *Raiders of the Lost Ark* was one of the very first Hollywood blockbuster movies released on home video.

At the time, I was working for a video rental chain in San Diego called Video Library. The local news media came to our main office to do an interview with Video Library's owner, Barry Rosenblatt, about the film's release.

Why did they come to us? Because Rosenblatt called them and let them know this news event was about to happen. We were all over the news in San Diego that week, and many customers were under the mistaken impression that we were the only chain that had the movie. That one bit of publicity brought us untold new customers who had never rented from us in the past, but became loyal customers.

Rules for Creating a Plan

As you can see, the use of objectives and strategies can make or break your business. When creating objectives and strategies, remember these two rules:

1. Set clear, concise, attainable, specific, measurable objectives with a goal and time limit. Don't forget accountability.
2. Describe in great detail the strategies you will use to reach each objective, and follow your plan to success.

List the steps that you'll take to create your plan, and keep a record of the actions taken to make it work. For example:

Step one:
Actions taken:

Step 6: How to
Position Your Business

What is positioning? Positioning is a perception of a product in the mind of your target market. How do you position your products in the minds of your target customers so they will buy it?

This is where your fortune will be made or lost. Let me explain it this way: If I were to ask you to name a brand of ketchup, most people would probably say Heinz. If I said soup, most people would say Campbell's. If I said Honda, most people would think automobile. If I said computer, most people would say IBM.

Copier, Xerox. Soft drink, Coke. Fast food, McDonald's. Etc.

When I say, "Name a brand of soup," for some people the store shelves may pop into their minds. For others, it might be a childhood memory of watching their mother make tomato soup and grilled cheese sandwiches, and picturing the soup can on the counter. For still others, it might be Andy Warhol's famous painting of the Campbell's soup can.

The result of positioning is what pops into the customer's mind about a product versus the competition. When I mention soup and you say Campbell's, suppose I go one step further and ask for a soup other than Campbell's. You might say Progresso, or Heinz. (Heinz? I thought they made ketchup.) If Campbell's is number one in the United States, it must be number one all over the world, right? Wrong! If you went to the United Kingdom, you would find that Heinz is the number one soup in England. So what's the problem here? Don't the Brits know good soup when they taste it? The two soups are the same here as they are in England, but the minds are different.

Another example:

If you went to Japan and told some Japanese acquaintances you had just bought a Honda, they would probably ask if it was your first motorcycle. In Japan, Honda is best known as a motorcycle company. Would you buy a Harley-Davidson automobile? Maybe? Would you buy Pennzoil cake mix? Betty Crocker tires? Buick cat food? How about an IBM lawn mower? Why not? They're good companies, aren't they?

Doesn't it make sense that IBM would make its lawn mowers with the same care and technology as its computers? If you saw the IBM lawn mower side by side with the Lawn-Boy, which would you feel more comfortable buying?

Are you beginning to see how powerful positioning can be? How you position your product can be the key to success or failure for your business. You bought this book because of how it was positioned by the publisher, or on the Small Town Marketing.Com web page, or in some other type of ad or promotion. You felt the unseen information was worth the price and made the investment.

So, if I have a soup company, is there no hope for me, because of Campbell's domination of the market? No, and that's the real beauty of positioning.

For this next example, I'm going to defer to a great book on this subject, and I suggest you run right out and buy it. It's called *Positioning: The Battle for Your Mind,* by Al Ries and Jack Trout (McGraw-Hill,

1981, 2001; Warner Books, 1986). It has the best examples of the next point I want to make: how to compete with the Campbell's soups and Heinz ketchups of the world. How this all relates to positioning in small towns will follow. But first, let's take a short history lesson.

Who's First?

In their book Ries and Trout ask, "Who was the first person to fly solo across the Atlantic Ocean?" Most of you should say, "Charles Lindbergh." Who was the second person to fly solo across the Atlantic Ocean? How quickly we forget the household name of . . . Bert Hinkler? Yes, good old Bert Hinkler. He flew the distance in a shorter time than Lindbergh and used less fuel. Who was the second person to walk on the moon? What is the second tallest mountain in the world? If you're second to your competitors, are you in deep trouble? No, and here's why.

Be First Where You Can Be

Ries and Trout's book goes on to point out, "Who was the third person to fly solo across the Atlantic Ocean?" If you didn't know the second person, how on earth could I imagine you would know the third? Well, you do. It was Amelia Earhart.

But even better for you, Amelia isn't remembered as the third person to fly solo across the Atlantic. She was what? Exactly; she was the first *woman* to fly solo across the Atlantic Ocean.

What this means is you can position yourself away from your competition into a category where you have less or no competition. Thanks to Al Ries and Jack Trout for pointing out what should be obvious.

I positioned my company, smalltownmarketing.com, as a place for businesses in small towns and/or small markets to go for business help, instead of just another marketing company on the Internet promising the same old stuff.

I searched the Internet extensively for any kind of marketing help for businesses in small towns and small markets, and found nothing. That doesn't mean there isn't any—just that I didn't find any. There are no books on Amazon.com or Barnesandnoble.com devoted to small town marketing. This will be the first.

Are We Alone?

So, for the time being I'm alone. As my success grows, more and more imitators will come along and try to lure market share from me. As that happens, just as with any business, my success will depend on how strong my position as the authority on small town marketing is in the minds of those who attend my seminars, visit my web site, or purchase my marketing books, articles, and newsletters.

Town versus City

What makes positioning in a small town so different than in a large metropolitan area?

Mostly two things:

First, in a small town, more people know you and may have already formed a perception of you before you even start your business. If this perception is that you don't know the business, you will have a challenge in this area.

If you buy a pizza business and have not been in the restaurant business in town before, people may give you the benefit of the doubt and support your business. Or, they may stay away because they think you couldn't possibly make a decent pizza due to your inexperience. They don't know that for four years at college you worked in a pizza parlor to support yourself, and while there you learned the pizza business, and that's why you bought the store in the first place.

Second, because positioning, by its very nature, is mind control of sorts, once people in your small town perceive you in a certain way, it is an uphill climb to change their minds. Plus, in a small town, word of mouth spreads rapidly.

If you position your product incorrectly in a large city, you have a large enough customer base to overcome that obstacle. You just reposition the product and continue on. In a small town the customer base is more limited, so once the damage is done, it's done. And so are you.

How do major businesses in the industry position themselves?

Set Yourself Apart

Let's go back to our baby products store for a moment. How do baby stores in large cities position themselves? Call some up and ask them. Where and how do they advertise? How do they set themselves apart from their competition? What are their strengths compared to their competitors?

You could position yourself as the baby expert store. Bring in pediatricians and other experts for seminars and workshops. Rent or sell videos on child rearing. Or maybe your store is the place to get those unusual baby things that ordinary stores don't carry—sort of the Sharper Image of baby products. How about the educational baby store for little geniuses?

Most small businesses make two major mistakes positioning their products:

First, they assume their customers think like them, act like them, and have the same interests and motives they have. They don't do the research necessary to identify their target market accurately. They advertise on radio or television stations they like, instead of the stations the target market is tuned to.

Try this experiment. For the next week, completely alter your lifestyle when it comes to radio, television, and newspapers. Listen to a radio station you've never listened to before. Watch TV shows you've never watched. Look and listen to who sponsors these shows. Are your competitors there? Are related businesses advertising there? Can you tell from the message which target market they are talking to? Can you see their ideal customer in your mind while listening to their message?

Second, they assume the consumer will compare similar products logically, and then make a decision based strictly on the merits and features of the product. But, as we know from our marketing research, people don't buy features; they buy benefits.

My first rule of advertising is based on this age-old advertising axiom: When logic and emotion come into conflict, emotion always wins. We make a buying decision based on how the product or service makes us feel emotionally; then we set out to create a logical argument to justify that emotional feeling. Do yourself a favor and take yourself out of the equation. Rely on facts that your market research has uncovered to reach the right people with the right message.

Once again, I can't stress enough the importance of the business resume in Step 1 of this marketing plan. Ask yourself every conceivable question about your business and its products. You must know your business and its market inside and out. Your positioning must be right on in a small town or small market. The smaller the town or market, the more difficult the task and there is virtually no margin for error.

Consider that studies have shown that the average number of people who attend a wedding or a funeral is 250. Your sphere of influence is 250 friends, neighbors, co-workers, and relatives. If you live in a town of 5,000, these people are 5 percent of the total population. If you have to reposition your products or services, start the process with these people. You need to encourage them to spread the word and neutralize any negative position.

Reflect Reality

There is one last, very important point I want to make about positioning. Positioning determines the kind of message your advertising is going to deliver to customers. We all want to show off our businesses in the best light possible. When we create an advertising message, it should reflect reality to our customers.

When people read your advertising, do they think they are coming to a premium steak house, only to discover that you are running a hamburger stand? If you are sending an embellished message to your customers, you are doing them and your business a great disservice. Don't expect your salespeople to sell customers who are disillusioned as soon as they walk in the door.

In today's business climate, it's extremely important to be honest in every area of your business. We've already established that you can't be all things to all people. You'll want to show your business to your customers as you see it, but when you walk in the front door of your business, make sure you see the same business your customer sees.

CHAPTER 8

How to Create an Advertising Plan in Your Own Backyard

The focus of this chapter is how business owners (including home-based businesses) in small towns and/or small markets can create their own advertising plans. As much as the so-called marketing experts would like to disagree with me, you and I both know that operating a business in a small town or small market is nothing like operating the same type of business in a large city. Take away the expert's multimillion-dollar advertising budget, and many Fortune 500 CEOs would have a hard time creating an ad campaign for the average small business.

Start by Knowing What Advertising Is

The first rule of advertising is: Advertising must always be an investment. It can never be an expense. Advertising must always produce more dollars in sales than it costs. Otherwise, why would you bother doing it?

Does advertising work immediately? Not always. Studies show that your customers must see your ad at least nine times before they consider yours a credible business. And, because they miss every third ad, you must run 27 ads in order for them to be exposed to the nine.

Depending on the size of your town, the size and type of ad, and the media available, you may be able to get by with less. Use the 27 ads as a rule of thumb until you know for sure. Also, keep in mind that we are not as interested in the cost per thousand of our advertising as we are in the cost per customer that it produces in revenue. Remember, you don't want your advertising to be an expense; you want it to be an investment.

You want to create a plan that is tailored to your business, while at the same time tailoring it to your individual small town or market. There are a thousand things that make each small town different. What works great in one may fail miserably in another.

Four Basic Advertising Questions

The first step in developing your advertising plan is asking yourself the following four questions.

1. *Why are you advertising?* What do you expect to happen? No one advertises just to see his or her name in print. Your advertising has to solve a problem in the customer's mind. Here is where you will use the objectives and strategies you developed in Chapter 6.

2. *Have you found your target market group of ideal customers?* You may have identified one or more groups of customers for the next step.

3. *What is your advertising message?* How are you going to convince customers that they need your products or services? Who are you going to speak to? What hot buttons can you push?

4. *Where and how often should you advertise?* What is the ideal medium to reach your target market? Will you use one medium or a combination?

By answering these four questions, you will begin to develop the direction your advertising will take. If you have a direction, you can set the necessary goals to make your campaign a success. Let's deal with these questions one at a time.

Why Are You Advertising?

Here is where you establish your advertising goals. What do you want your advertising to accomplish? For example, yours might be a new business and you just need to get the word out. Or you may want to attempt to steal customers from your competition. You may want your advertising to reinforce your business in the minds of current customers and retain their loyalty. And last, but not least, you may want to promote a sale for immediate profits.

You may want your advertising to do all of these things, or even more that I haven't listed. The point is: Before you can create any ad campaign, you need to have a goal of what you want that advertising to accomplish.

Once you have your goals, prioritize them. Advertising works best when you develop these goals one at a time.

Have You Found Your Target Market Group of Ideal Customers?

Once again, advertising has major advantages in small towns. Advertising directed at everybody rarely succeeds. Great advertising is directed at one person. Pick your very best customer and tailor your message directly to that person. Your customers should tell you, "When I heard your ad, I thought you were talking directly to me."

Needs and Desires   Customers rarely buy products and services they don't need. Are you confident you have identified the specific benefits that customers want and that you provide? Have you addressed how you can fill their needs better than someone else? How you present your products in your advertising will go a long way in deciding which medium to use (a subject that is covered in the next chapter).

What Is Your Advertising Message?

Here is where advertising in a small town becomes more complicated. If yours is a new business, you have some work ahead of you. If small town people don't know you, they are sometimes a little skeptical at first. It takes a little time for them to warm up to you.

If yours is an established business, people in your town may have formed a perception of who and what they think you are. Unlike people in big cities, residents of small towns talk to each other. They will carry your message, right or wrong.

If you want to make a change or modify your products or services, you may find the going a little tough. Customers in small towns tend to rely on first impressions. They create a perception of your business in their minds and that is pretty much how they are going to continue to see you.

It's not easy to change a mind that's already made up. In previous chapters, I discussed how people do not buy products based on comparing the facts and making a logical decision. People buy products based on emotional perception of how the product or service makes them feel. Have you addressed feelings in your advertising plan? What emotional tack will your advertising take? Your customers will get an emotional response from your advertising message, then create a logical argument in their minds that supports that response. If your advertising only presents the logical facts about your product, you should reread the position and target market chapters.

Where and How Often Should You Advertise?

The next chapter discusses in detail where and when to advertise. In this chapter, a better question would be, "Where should I *not* advertise?" The answer to that question is: "Don't advertise anywhere unless your target market is there." If you aren't reaching your target market, you are wasting your advertising dollars.

How often you advertise will be determined by the success of your ads and by your budget. If your plan is designed correctly, advertising should pay for itself. It should produce more income than it costs. If it is designed incorrectly, you won't be able to do it for long, because it suddenly becomes an expense.

How to Set a Monthly Advertising Budget Most small business owners have no formal advertising budget in place. As a result, there is no intelligent allocation of funds to cover sales, emergencies, and other unexpected events. Jeff Delvaux is director of sales for the six-station Des Moines Radio Group in Des Moines, Iowa. Each of Delvaux's salespeople works with 100 to 200 clients per month. Here are his ideas for creating a radio advertising budget for a typical retail store that sells with a markup of 100 percent. There are six steps:

1. Delvaux starts with an idea by famous ad guru Roy Williams. If your business is in a high-rent district like a mall or a downtown location with lots of foot traffic, consider the value of rent in your ad plan. Start by taking 12 percent of projected retail sales for the next year and subtract your rent. If you are in a location where people need to search to find you, do not subtract your rent.

2. Next, determine your ad budget. Twelve percent of $1 million in projected gross sales for the coming year would be $120,000. Subtract $70,000 in rent, leaving $50,000 as your ad budget for the year.

3. How to spend it? Jeff suggests allocating 50 percent of the $50,000 ($25,000) over the next 12 months, based on sales from the previous year. For example, if you did 10 percent of your total yearly sales in July, you would allocate 10 percent of $25,000 ($2,500) to July advertising. If you did 20 percent of total sales for the year in December, then you would allocate 20 percent of $25,000 ($5,000) to December. Each month would have advertising money as a percentage of sales from the previous year, so allocations for all months would add up to 100 percent.

4. Using this method, you will have advertising funds available every month of the year. But you would also like to have a sale every quarter, and that will require extra capital for sale ads in those months. So, allocate 25 percent of your total budget for sales. That would be $12,500 annually (25 percent of $50,000), or an additional $3,125 per quarter, that will be added to the money already allocated to those months in the preceding step.

5. So far you have used 75 percent of your ad budget—50 percent divided over the months of the year, and 25 percent for sales. Next, allocate 15 percent to the "O" in SWOT—opportunities. These opportunities are going to arise sooner or later, and with this plan, you will have $7,500 available to take advantage of them when they do—even if you are having a sale at the same time.

6. Last but not least, the remaining 10 percent will go into an emergency fund. If you need a little extra for Christmas advertising, you will have it. Or, if it's not needed, you can blow it on a company party or give it to charity.

Here is the radio ad budget summary:

- Fifty percent allocated to general advertising, spread over 12 months according to the percentage of monthly sales from the previous year.

- Twenty-five percent for sales.
- Fifteen percent for opportunities.
- Ten percent for emergencies, bonuses, or fun things.

Will this plan work? On paper it should. But, in order for it to be effective for you, it will require some very strict discipline. You will always have half your ad budget sitting there in a nice fat fund waiting, and the temptation to use it might be too much for some business owners. No plan is going to work for you unless you follow it to the letter.

Final Thoughts on Small Town Advertising Plans

As you can see, small town advertising is a little different animal than advertising in cities. It's like an aquarium. The larger the aquarium (i.e., the large city), the more mistakes you can make and the fish survive. The smaller the aquarium, the fewer mistakes it will tolerate before the fish die.

Another small town problem is testing your marketing or advertising. In small towns your competitors are very aware of everything you do. They can react to counter your successful advertising very quickly.

The most important areas to concentrate on are to accurately define your target market and customers, know your town and its idiosyncrasies, know your product and its benefits, and know your local media and how to use them. No one said it would be easy; but no one said it would be impossible, either.

Advertising: Learn from the Mistakes of Others

When it comes to the competition, one of the principles I teach is not to obsess about them, but be aware of what they are doing . . . or *not* doing. When was the last time you really looked at the advertising messages of your competitors? I mean really looked?

Don't just look at what they have on sale, but try to see what is the real message of their ads. Chances are there isn't one. The reason a clear message is missing is because the ad was created or generated by someone who didn't really know the vision or direction of the company. Most ads simply report information (mostly sales), without really grabbing the customer's attention or interest and creating a genuine need.

Advertising has two, and only two, functions: to inform the consumer and to issue a call to action. What do you see when you look at your competitors' ads? Is there anything to inspire the customer to act? Is there a real call to action? In most cases, customers will go right past their ad without a second thought, unless they have an overpowering need for the product.

Did you ever notice how many tire ads there are in the newspaper? Not unless you need tires. But when you decide that it's the right time to buy tires, the ads suddenly seem to be everywhere. That's just the first part of successful advertising. Shouldn't the ad make you get up, go out to the garage, and look at your tires? Shouldn't the ad make you think about the product or service before the actual need arises? In the preceding paragraph, I said one of the purposes of advertising is to inform the customer. That includes creating a need in their minds as you inform them about your products and services.

Here are some common mistakes your competitors are probably making. Learn from them.

Trying to Do Too Much with Too Little

Business owners often tell me that they can't wait for the day their business is established and they don't have to advertise so much. Let me tell you, that day should never come. I don't think it has arrived yet for McDonald's or Wendy's. You can't be all things to all people, so don't advertise everywhere. Focus your efforts where your target market is located, and ignore the rest.

Advertising Based Only on Cost

Where is the lowest-priced place for me to advertise? Advertising representatives will tell you that cost per thousand is the most important consideration. However, it's not cost per thousand, but cost per customer that you should be considering. If your advertising is working, the cost is free. The increase in customer traffic and sales should more than offset the cost of advertising.

Advertising Infrequently

New businesses often run one or two ads and declare, "Advertising just doesn't work for us; we've tried it." As mentioned earlier, research says we need to see an ad at least nine times in order for the company to be creditable in our eyes. The problem is we usually miss every third ad. To reach the average person nine times, we actually have to run the ad a minimum of 27 times for it to be seen at least nine times.

Using Large Ads

Size doesn't always count. In the yellow pages, the larger the ad, the more it pulls. This is not always true in small towns, though, and I address this topic in the next chapter. In other types of advertising, it also isn't always the case. Consistent messages, in size and content, usually do better over time than running big, then small, ads.

Trying to Win an Award

Do you want your ad to sell product or win awards? Naturally you want the best possible ad you can afford. But don't let the messenger overpower the message. The message is the reason for the ad. It's expensive to have customers admire your ads but miss the message.

Imitating a Competitor

Don't be a me-too business to your customer. Your job is to set yourself apart from the competition, not imitate them. In Chapter 6, I explained how to use positioning to separate yourself from your competitors.

Failing to Capitalize on Strengths

You should know the demographics of your target market. What product strengths can you match to them? Use your business's strong points to overcome competitive disadvantages.

No Advertising Measurement

How effective is your advertising? How do you measure what your ads produce? You must develop procedures to measure whether the ad is doing the job. One way is to key your ads. You need some signal that will alert you to where the customer came from. For example: If the customer calls and asks for a free copy of "Ten Things You Should Know Before You Buy Tires," you would know that's from your newspaper ad.

On radio you may tell the customer to call and "Ask for Joe." On TV it's "Ask for Steve." In magazines, it's "Ask for Pete." Put codes on all coupon ads to tell you what papers they came from. A code such as (BC210/08) might mean the *Bozeman Chronicle* (BC) the second week (2) of October 2008 (10/08). The number of coupons you redeem will tell you how effective the ad is. You can't evaluate the medium unless you know which one the coupons came from.

Advertising Is Not a Cure-All

If you have a lousy business, poor customer service, or bad products, all the great ads in the world won't help you. Advertising can't overcome business weaknesses. Fix the business before you waste your advertising dollars putting out the wrong message to the right people.

I'm sure I don't have to tell you that advertising is expensive enough when it works, and even worse when it doesn't. If you use these tips, you can save yourself some valuable ad dollars and improve your advertising efforts.

CHAPTER 9

Step 7: What Do We Say, How Do We Say It, and Where Do We Say It?

I n order to develop your advertising and promotion strategies, you have a few more questions that need to be answered. The previous six steps of the marketing plan have been designed to assemble the information needed to create the advertising message that will reach your target market.

Before starting, I suggest that you do one more reading of the information you gathered for each of the previous six steps. Have you included everything in your business resume? What about your SWOT analysis—has anything changed? Are you sure you've defined your target market and secondary markets? Do you feel comfortable with your objectives and strategies to achieve your goals? Have you positioned your business for your target market? As Davy Crockett said, "Be always sure you're right—then go ahead." If this quote fits your plan at this point, then go ahead.

Products or Services: What Are You Selling?

There are six areas of business that deal with your product or service: tangibility, product name, comparison, pricing, delivery, and customer contact. You need to define them and decide whether you will or won't use them in your advertising.

I'll discuss the products and services first, then the message and how to deliver it.

Tangible or Intangible?

When we purchase a TV or an automobile, there is a tangible item at the end of the transaction. Tangible products are those we can see, touch, taste, and sometimes smell. Most salespeople assume it's easier to sell a product if the customer can both see and touch the item. Things like size, weight, or color often add to the value of a product in the mind of the customer, so keep those thoughts in mind when creating your advertising message if you are selling a tangible product.

Intangible products are unseen or unable to be touched—for example, insurance or clean carpets (you can touch the carpets, but you can't touch the fact that they are clean).

Intangible products are almost always produced by service businesses. If you have an intangible product, your description in your advertising must create a picture in the prospects' minds, because you don't have a product they can touch. Using insurance again, the message is peace of mind that insurance will provide for the family in case of emergency or loss of a loved one. Carpet cleaning will produce a clean environment for the family. Legal services will protect someone's rights concerning property or monetary issues.

Intangible products or services are emotional, not logical. By that I mean that customers will buy on a gut feeling provided by such things as the advertising message, company credibility, or even their impression about the integrity of the salesperson. There aren't two products your customers can lay down side by side and evaluate. If they are considering carpet cleaning, they will, more than likely, make their decision based on the company they feel comfortable with and they think can do the best job, rather than the one that is the cheapest.

Promote Both the Product and the Emotion   Michelin sells a tangible product (tires), but uses infants in its commercials to promote an intangible (how safe customers will feel with Michelin tires on their car). The advertising message hits two markets. First, Michelin promotes the quality of its tires with the safety message; then, they add the emotional factor with the same message. Customers who want either safety or quality (or both) will at least consider Michelin tires.

Who Are You?   Once again, you need to return to Step 1 and Step 2 of the marketing plan and look for the strengths that need to be included in your message. Are you going to include pictures or testimonials of the staff, management, or customers in your ads? Should experience be included? Is there anything I, as a customer, need to know about you that will influence my buying decision?

If you are selling an intangible product, these options work very well. Seeing your staff in pictures makes the company seem more human. Customers can see the actual people they will be dealing with. They might even recognize some of them.

Remember, you are trying to build customer confidence in the company or the brand name. Any information about your company and its employees that reduces the anxiety in the customer's mind will be a plus, and will move you closer to the sale.

What's in a Name?

If you are introducing a new product, there's a need to create a brand image. Tide, Xerox, IBM, and Apple all spend tremendous amounts of money on promoting and keeping their brand names at the front of your mind. The reason we think of these brands first is due to the constant bombardment of their names by advertising, day in and day out.

One of the most successful builders of brand names in the world today is Procter & Gamble (P&G). There never would have been a P&G if William Procter, a candle maker, and James Gamble, a soap maker, had not married sisters. Starting as a home-based business in 1837, they built an empire over the years, so that today 23 of P&G's brands have more than a billion dollars in annual sales, and another 18 have sales between $500 million and $1 billion.

Tide, Pampers, Charmin, Crest, Bounce, Gillette, Old Spice, Folgers, Right Guard, and Duracell are all brand names P&G has turned into household names. Will we forget these names if we don't hear about them day in and day out? You bet we will.

Has it been awhile since you thought about Ipana toothpaste? Bucky Beaver, its mascot? If you are under the age of 40, the chances are you've never even heard of Ipana toothpaste. It was a major brand name in the 1950s, and was a major TV advertiser. Now it's sold only in one or two Midwestern states. If you can build a successful brand name, it will go a long way in paving your road to success.

Look at your competitors. How have they positioned their brand names? Are you going to be a second or third choice of the customer? Or are you going to position your name in a different category or in a different way?

There are other things to consider about your brand name. Which is more important—what you sell or who you are? Procter & Gamble is less well known than most of its brands. Did you know Oral-B tooth care products are owned by P&G?

What about complicated brand names? There is a dry cleaner in town called Persnickety Dry Cleaners. Do you know how to spell "Persnickety"? Would you be praying for a sign somewhere when making out your check? Would www.persnicketydrycleaners.com be an easy web site to find? There are many things to consider when it comes to branding a company name.

Don't Judge a Book by Its Cover Did you ever buy a book or magazine based on the cover or the hype and discovered afterward it was not what you expected? Brand names are certainly important, but so is something else—packaging. The physical look of the product can make it or, in some cases, break it. Chances are you picked up this book because the cover (packaging), or its wording, caught your eye.

Look at a box of Tide, for example. There is tangible and intangible packaging, just like the products or services mentioned on the previous pages. Let's see what we can discover.

How Do Customers Compare Products?

When P&G packages that box of Tide, which will be displayed next to its competitors' products, how the boxes of Tide look next to its competition becomes critical. Color, type styles, and design are some of the major components that attract customers to the product. The Tide logo design is no accident. Every part of it is designed to appeal to the emotions. Let's examine it more closely.

The Tide logo is the brand name, in bright blue (a calming or cool color), in front of an orange and yellow bull's-eye. Red, orange, and yellow are commonly referred to as "hot" colors or "buying" colors. Think McDonald's, Wendy's, and Burger King, to name just three.

The logo and the advertising messages on the Tide box cause customers to evaluate the product emotionally and/or logically. They make a purchase, or they return the Tide box to the shelf and buy a competitor's brand.

Now, you might want to make the case that Tide has been around forever, and that's why it still sells well. I would counter with the argument that Tide, through smart marketing and advertising, shot to the top and stayed there through the generations since its introduction in 1943 because of the emotional feeling that Tide will get clothes cleaner than any other brand. And that argument overcomes almost any other, including price.

Intangible Packaging   The best place to see examples of intangible packaging is in the yellow pages. Here, similar competitors are all displayed together, and studies show that the bigger the ad, the more response that ad gets—except in small towns. I'll cover what you need to know about the yellow pages in more detail shortly.

Pick a section of the yellow pages and study it.

The largest ads are usually those of personal injury attorneys. They are half-page to full-page ads. How do the attorneys position themselves? How do they set themselves apart from their competition? What points do they stress? You don't need complicated logos, fancy type styles, or electric colors in the yellow pages, as you would in other advertising. Keep it simple, but make it effective.

If you're not sure of your designs, bring in a group of family members or customers, and ask them to evaluate sample ads and packaging ideas. Ask them what they like, or don't like, about each one. Make a checklist of several points. "On a scale of 1 to 10, what do you think of . . . ?" Don't ask which one they like best. You'll just put undue pressure on them that there may be a right or wrong answer hidden somewhere. Make it as easy as possible to be honest and anonymous. They will provide more information if they feel they will remain unknown. I like to ask questions in the form of a survey.

They can add written information if they like, but I like to use check boxes that cover the pros and cons of what they are evaluating.

Does Pricing Belong in Advertising?

Are you going to include pricing in your advertising? In special sales and promotions, maybe yes. As a general rule, probably not. Why? When there is only price, with no described benefit or perceived value, customers become skeptical.

When I worked as a sales associate at Circuit City, a large electronics retailer, in the video department, we had a sale that started every Thursday and ended every Sunday. We always had a low-priced sale on TVs, CD players, camcorders, and the like. Normally referred to as loss leaders, these are products that are sold well below cost, and their sole purpose is to generate customer traffic to the department. Customers would come in and ask to see the sale item. The first question was usually something like "What's wrong with it?" or "How come it's so cheap?"

It's illegal for companies to engage in bait-and-switch tactics, meaning to lure the customer into the store with the promise of a low-priced advertised product that is usually out of stock. Then, the salesperson tries to switch the customer to a higher-priced and more profitable product.

The department rule at Circuit City was "Show, tell, and offer to sell." In other words, show customers the product, truthfully tell them about it, and ask them for the order. If they didn't buy it, or they asked about another product, then you were off the hook as far as bait and switch was concerned. But if they insisted on the advertised product, you had to sell them that product or a comparably priced item at the sale price.

The point I want to stress here is that you can live or die by price. In most cases, your business is going to die if you try to be the low-priced leader in your market area. In order to be competitive, you are going to have to rely on volume sales; that means higher inventory costs, less affluent customers, collection problems, and more work for the salesperson. And that will almost always result in higher employee turnover and, unfortunately, less profit in the long run.

If I told you I had a product for sale and the price was a bargain at $200, would you say, "Sounds terrific, I'll take it!"? Chances are you would not. You would probably want just a little more information before you parted with your hard-earned 200 bucks for some mystery product. So, there are considerations other than price.

When customers are uninformed about particular products or services, price is often the only way they feel they can evaluate product differences. The ones that cost more are probably better in some way, and the cheaper ones are lower in quality. The only way to battle price is to give the customer information that will put the product's price in the proper perspective.

Price must be attached to real customer benefits before it becomes a consideration. Every feature of a product is useless unless it has a corresponding benefit to the customer. Benefits justify price and create value.

Pay close attention; this next point is extremely important. If the feature is not a benefit to the customer, then it is simply useless information. The more useless features, the more expensive the item becomes in the mind of the customer. Why pay for features you are not going to use or need? It's like waterproof shoes in Death Valley. Does that feature (waterproofing) create more or less value in the product? Do you want to pay for that feature? Or would you like to compare it to the shoes that don't have waterproofing? That's what makes finding out what the customer really needs (from Chapter 4 on sales) so crucial to your sales success.

The more benefits the product has that are needed or desired by the buyer, the less consideration there is about price, and the more valuable the product becomes in the eyes of the consumer. Each time the perception of value increases, concern about the price decreases, and the product becomes more desirable.

How Do You Get Your Products or Services to the Customer?

Once you sell your product, you must get it to the customer. Is shipping or delivery a plus, or a minus, to the customer? And how do you say that in your ad? Does the customer pick it up? Does it have to be shipped? Mailed? Delivered? FedEx? UPS? How does your distribution stack up against that of your competitors? Are you faster? Slower? Cheaper? More expensive? Does the product need to be installed once it's delivered? Does it need special handling? Is it sensitive to temperature?

All customers expect a timely delivery of the product. In the furniture business, I would much rather sell furniture in stock than special order it. A special order can, and often does, take six to eight weeks—up to two full months. When selling an in-stock item, the sale is completed almost immediately. The delivery is scheduled, and the customer has seen what he or she is going to receive. With special orders, there is time for customers to find something they like better and cancel the sale. If they already have the merchandise, there is much less chance of a cancellation. Effective distribution is a huge customer sales plus. The more effective you are at delivering the product, the better your business will be.

Who Contacts the Customer?

Are you going to use direct selling in your business? In other words, will a commission salesperson sell the product to a customer one-on-one? Or do customers order it by catalog, or buy off the shelf at your location? Is it sold on the Internet? Is it a self-service operation? What selling aids do your salespeople need? Catalogs, price lists, computers, order forms, travel, and so on—you must consider all the costs related to these selling activities.

Many car dealer ads tout the length of time their salespeople have been with them. For many people, length of service is a positive. They feel they will be better taken care of by someone experienced.

Some people are uncomfortable with salespeople. They would rather look on their own. They often feel that they will be tricked into buying, or will be shown products the salesperson wants to sell, rather than what the customer really needs. However, if you have a crack sales staff, talk about them on your web site and in your advertising. In many cases, the crack sales staff will be you. If you have a very satisfied customer, ask for a testimonial and get permission to use it in your ads.

What are your sales strategies? Remember the Victor Business Machines story? Seventy-five cold calls, 20 machine placements, five sales. That was its sales strategy. Do your salespeople need to be certified or licensed? Will they need special training at schools or seminars?

Reaching the customer is the focus. If we can't sell the customer, the business is destined for failure.

Rule of Two

Fred E. Hahn and Kenneth G. Mangun, in their book, *Do-It-Yourself Advertising and Promotion* (John Wiley & Sons, 1997), define the Rule of Two and the Rule of Three.

The Rule of Two simply says, "See an ad once, it's a test; see it twice, it's a success." Document all the places your competitors' ads are running. Keep a pad handy, and make a note when you see one of your competitors' ads on television or hear one on radio. What time of day do the ads run? Which TV or radio shows do your competitors sponsor? Cut out and save competitors' newspaper and magazine ads by month. If they start to advertise anywhere on a consistent basis, they must be getting some return on investment (ROI) from the ads; otherwise, why would the ads be there?

How Much Attention Should You Give Competitors? Don't become obsessed with your competitors' messages. Their company goals may be completely different from yours. Keeping an eye on your competition is like watching the opposing team's game films. It's not so much what they are doing, but what you can learn from what they are doing. What can you do better? What can you exploit?

You don't want your competitors to dictate how and where you advertise, but there are some things to look for. Monitor your competitors' ads and look for a response request. Is there a call to action in their ads?

"Half off!" does not qualify as a call to action. "Bring in this coupon and get half off all weekend!" is a call to action designed to bring customers to their location. If there is no call to action, how can your competitor know the ad's drawing power?

Key your ads. (I'll cover how to do this in greater detail later.) In a nutshell, keying your ads means that the "call to action" message in that ad will let you know which medium the ad came from. It might be a code number printed in a corner of a coupon, or "Ask for John" or "Ask for extension 200" for a phone call.

Using this method, you can evaluate the power of the ad and decide if it's worth running again. Don't waste advertising money by running ads that don't pull customers. If you're running a new series of ads, make sure you allow enough time between ads to evaluate the effectiveness of the campaign.

Rule of Three

According to Hahn and Mangun, the Rule of Three says that an ad message must appear three times in a medium that is seen or read by the same audience before you can expect it to be noticed once. Studies show that it takes nine impressions of an ad before people have the confidence to try your business.

Applying the Rule of Three and the nine impressions, you will need to run your ad 27 times before it becomes effective. This type of advertising is useful in name recognition advertising. It also explains why advertising doesn't always work immediately, and why you need to pay attention to the Rule of Two.

Not Sure Where to Advertise?

Most public and university libraries have Standard Rate and Data Service (SRDS) directories. They are guides to the full range of options on advertising to a specific audience or in a particular field. They contain detailed information, field by field, on nearly every medium that accepts advertising. For more information, check the SRDS web site at www.srds.com; write SRDS at 1700 Higgins Road, Des Plaines, IL 60018-5605; or call (847) 375-5000.

Next, the Message: Who Do You Talk to and How Do You Say It?

Have you ever wondered what makes a great ad? John McWade is the founder of PageLab in Sacramento, California, and the first desktop publishing studio. Here are 10 things he looks for:

1. *We all like surprises.* Can you state an ordinary message in an unusual way? Commercials done differently are the ones we talk about at work the next day.
2. *Keep it simple.* Don't let the design overpower the message. The idea is the most important part of the message.

3. *Get me involved*. Shock me, make me mad, make me happy, make me cry, but don't bore me and leave me cold.

4. *Make me curious*. Isn't the real purpose of an ad to make me want more information? Grab my attention and hold it.

5. *Great ads command answers*. They demand that you respond to the ad. They are like an unanswered question that must be resolved.

6. *Draw your own conclusion*. Isn't the strongest conclusion the one we draw ourselves? An ad that brings me to a conclusion is powerful indeed.

7. *The headline and the image tell the story*. The headline should never tell you what is in the picture, only what you *don't* see. The headline and picture together create the story.

8. *They never brag*. Yellowstone Harley-Davidson in Belgrade, Montana, has a billboard at the edge of town that proclaims, "The Largest Harley-Davidson Dealer in Belgrade!" (Belgrade is a town of 3,000 to 4,000 people.) It also is the only dealer in over a hundred miles. That's just a fact of life, not bragging at all.

9. *Great ads are always well executed*. They have good design that doesn't overpower the message. They have sharp photos, good typefaces, and so on.

10. *They sell*. The most important function of any ad is to sell. What good is an ad that wins award after award if it doesn't sell?

Apply the Rules

You know your target market and you know your product. Next, you've got to create a message that will reach and appeal to your target at a cost that's within your budget. Let's look at the five most popular methods of getting the message out: promotion, direct mail, advertising, Internet, and publicity.

Promotion

The first order of business is goals. As with everything else I talk about in this book, you have to know what you want your promotion to accomplish. You can't begin to decide how to promote if you don't have an expectation of the end result. Perhaps you expect to bring X number of customers into the business the first week or month or X number of phone inquiries. If you establish a goal, it's much easier to create the promotion.

Promotion is one area where being in a small town is an advantage to business. You are reaching a small area, and, even though you have competition, you have less than in most large cities. If you are in a larger community, you need to define the area you want to draw from. Next, you identify the methods of reaching your target market in this area.

You should have a certain amount of money allocated to advertising and promotion in your business plan. I cover this money allocation later on in the book. Your business may live or die depending on how you spend this money.

Getting Started   To promote your business, there is a host of things you can do. Coupons, contests and sweepstakes, sales, or rebates all should increase traffic to your business if they are presented to the right people. Which one or combination you use depends on the goals you set on what you want the promotion to accomplish, and which promotion will accomplish the goal most economically.

New Business?   If you are a new business, the first item of business is the promotion of a grand opening. I think every retail business should have an annual grand opening. New people move to town, and they will not know about you or your business. Established residents will begin to look forward to your yearly event and promote it for you by word of mouth.

Dealing with the Media   Contact the local media about your grand opening three to six months before your opening and see what advertising options are available to you. The one hard-and-fast rule you must keep in mind is that whatever medium you choose must reach your target market. Cost should not be the final deciding factor. If a form of advertising reaches your customer it should be strongly considered.

Is your store opening a news event? Have you made your business unique in some way? Television stations may want to cover your opening or at least do a story about the business. Radio stations love to do live remotes at new businesses, but are usually not free.

A feature article in the newspaper about your new business is worth much more than any grand opening ad. Many newspapers have a "People in Business" section where you can put a small announcement about your business. It's not always easy to reach these media people and convince them you are genuine news and not trying to con them into doing some free publicity for you.

If they do decide to do an article about your business, I would strongly consider buying some ad space anyway. Just because they say they are going to do the article is no guarantee that the editor might not pull the story.

Newspapers, TV magazines, and radio usually have reduced rates for new or first-time advertisers. You may need to commit to a certain number of ads or spots to get the reduced rates.

Established Business?   If you are an established business, you have established customers. Build your business on them. Have a special or private sale or event for these customers who have supported you over the years. Show them that you appreciate their support, and they will promote your business for you. A referral from an existing customer is the most powerful type of business contact.

"John Smith sent me in" is much more powerful than "I saw your ad in the *Daily Journal*." Remember, your good name is what your business survives on in the long haul. It's impossible to place a value on this kind of promotion.

Direct Mail

One of the least expensive ways to get your message out in a small town is direct mail. The first order of business is to create a mailing list.

You could purchase a list from a mailing list broker, but this is sometimes prohibitive for a small town because you need to purchase a minimum number of names.

I did a promotion for a local spa dealer. One of the criteria I needed was an annual income of at least $80,000. The listing company had a 3,000-name minimum at a price of $55 per thousand. To get enough names with that income I had to expand the list to include five other counties.

Because of distance and servicing costs, the spa company would sell in only two of those counties. It was necessary to purchase a lot of names the spa dealer would never use, just to get the names in Bozeman and the surrounding area. The cost of a little over $170 might seem like a waste of money, but it was faster than creating a specialized list, which I'll cover next.

Check at the Chamber of Commerce and the Post Office   Pick up a membership directory from your local chamber of commerce and create a mailing list. Sit down and hand type the mailing label information into MS Word or Excel. Many chambers already have a list in mailing label form they sell. If you can't afford that, make your own from the chamber directory.

You can also get mailing lists from the post office. You can buy postal carrier routes for specific neighborhoods. You can send post-cards (26 cents each = $26 per 100 postcards) or letters/brochures (41 cents each = $41 per 100) to specific neighborhoods announcing your grand opening.

What about bulk mail? Isn't it less expensive than a first class mailing? Yes, it is, but there are some strong disadvantages to bulk mail, especially in larger cities.

The first disadvantage is bulk mail is not always delivered in a timely manner by the post office. It is included with other mail as volume permits. It could possibly be delivered after your grand opening is over.

The second disadvantage is that customers look through the mail over the wastebasket, and many bulk mail letters go directly into the trash without even being opened. That's why I like sending postcards first class.

The rates for first class postcards are almost the same as bulk mail rates, and the postcards are delivered with other first class mail. If you include "Address Correction Requested" under the return address, the post office will update your mailing list free.

Another reason I prefer postcards is they can be made to look different each time. A letter is a letter with a different teaser on the outside.

A final advantage for postcards is that they are almost always read by more than just the person to whom they are addressed.

Key Your Postcards   Give customers a reason to keep the postcard and bring it in later. As a key to your mailings, ask them to bring the postcard as an entry to a sweepstakes or drawing for free gifts. Keep the mailing lists, and mail to these people two to three times over the next six to eight months. Why? Because you need to develop a name recognition relationship with your customers.

Name Recognition   If your business is brand-new, you need customers to learn your name and associate it with your business as soon as possible. If they see your name only once, how are they going to remember your business? We remember names and businesses because of the perceived benefits they provide us. How many people have you met one time and remembered their names? I'll bet there are only a few. It's the same with your business. The customer needs to hear your name over and over to reinforce the name in their minds.

Advertising Message

What's your advertising message? When I talk about advertising, I am talking about two basic concepts. Advertising informs and/or persuades your customers to do something. If you're a new business, you will use both concepts. Inform (name recognition/product existence) and persuade (a call to action) the customer to consider the purchase of your product or service.

Advertising Objectives   Just like your sales objectives, you need to set advertising goals and objectives. What will your advertising accomplish? How long will it take? What will it cost? What type of strategy are you going to use?

Who Benefits?   What benefit will the target market receive from your product? What problem will be solved? What assurance can you offer that the risk of trying or using your product will be minimal? When I shop at an unfamiliar business, there are several criteria I use.

First, I have to evaluate any protections I have in dealing with this business. Does it carry brand names? Does it offer service and a guarantee or warranty on its products? Does it have a return policy? Are there charges for any of these protections, such as restocking fees?

Second, how am I treated in the store? Do the employees care that I'm there? Do I feel comfortable with their knowledge of their products? Is the store well stocked? If it's a professional office, is it clean and professional looking?

Oh, What a Feeling!   What is the feeling your advertising conveys to the customer? For example, if I'm selling used cars, I may do a lot of exclaiming about our great weekend car sale. If I'm from a funeral parlor, I'm going to have a much more subdued and refined delivery. I'm not going to yell about our weekend casket sale. Successful advertising involves not only what is said, but how you say it.

How to Execute   If you're spearheading the advertising yourself, there are six things you need to be aware of.

1. *How are your logos and business name presented?* All your ads, brochures, TV spots, radio should maintain a certain family resemblance. If I see your ads in the newspaper or yellow pages, I should see a similar look (colors, layout, type styles, etc.). On TV or radio I should hear your trademark music or familiar voice.

2. *Are legal disclaimers required?* How are they shown in the ad? Insurance, real estate, and financial planners have to include certain legal wording in all their ads.

3. *What product lines are included?* Does the customer need to be educated about your line? If you have a new line of vacuum cleaners, would it help sell me if I saw it in action? What does an iPod do, and why do I need one? What will blue tooth technology do for me?

4. *Store name, phone, address, web site, and so on?* Where do the store name, phone number, street address, web site address, and other basic information appear? How large are they? If your ad is doing its job, the customer is going to be looking for this information. Don't let the message overpower it. Don't make me get a magnifying glass to find your phone number.

5. *Colors? Typefaces?* All are important parts of your ads' family resemblance. Where will your ads be placed in your medium of choice?

6. *Co-op advertising?* This is a common practice in advertising. A company will pay part of the cost of advertising if you feature

their products in the ad. How are the sponsoring companies' logos used? What hoops do you have to jump through to get your co-op money? Your advertising goals and target market information will make it easier to decide on the type of media to use to get your message out.

How to Choose the Best Media Mix for Your Message   In a small town, you should begin by analyzing all local media choices available to you. This can be both good and bad. New business owners are often tempted to advertise in all available media. They use the shotgun approach, thinking, "If I take a shotgun and shoot at the entire human race, some of the pellets are bound to hit my customer." Smart advertisers will use the rifle approach to zero in on their target market.

Everything, from the local newspaper to a spot in the back of the high school yearbook, is fair game. After all, that's one of the reasons it's called a target market.

You want to get the message out, but your advertising budget is probably limited and you must be smart in how and where your message is presented. Remember our rule: Advertising must be an investment rather than an expense. As your company grows, more advertising options will be open to you.

For now, let's concentrate on the basics. As I mentioned earlier, you want your advertising to have a family resemblance. In other words, your newspaper ads should resemble your brochure and other print ads. Unseen ads like radio should use the same phrasing as the newspaper and brochure. Over time your customers will begin to identify certain words and sounds with your company. These little snippets of information are the keys to keeping your company in the forefront of the customer's mind. It's why companies use slogans like "You deserve a break today" or "Where's the beef?"

Each time an ad is exposed to one of your customers it should be constantly reinforced by another ad in another medium. The customer starts to feel comfortable with the message and remembers it.

Let's discuss four points you must deal with when choosing where to put your messages.

1. You want to be noticed by the largest segment of your target market. From the target market section of the plan you should have a fairly accurate idea by now of who your target market is. The questions then become: What percentages listen to radio, read newspapers, and so on? If enough customers listen to KABC radio, it might make good sense to consider that station for your advertising budget.

2. Use your advertising dollars in the most economical way. For example, you might use television as a short-time medium to promote your grand opening. But the cost of TV might be prohibitive for your day-to-day advertising.

3. You may have primary and secondary target markets. You need to be sure that the media you choose will reach the key groups within your total target market. Keep in mind that you might use the rock station to reach young customers while the easy listening station would bring in the older customers.

4. When using different media, you must stay on top of your advertising. Be sure there is consistency of image about your business. Make sure your spots are running when they're supposed to and with the correct message.

Radio and television stations are required to give you an itemized bill as to what commercials ran and when. If they don't, then insist on it or pull your advertising. Discovering that your sale ad began running after the sale was over is a poor use of your advertising budget.

Frequency, Reach, Impressions, Rating Points—What Do They All Mean? Every industry has its buzzwords. Frequency, reach, impressions, and rating points are the jargon of radio, television, and newsprint. Each term is very important to the success of your advertising. It's worth the time to at least learn their definitions as you work toward selecting your advertising medium of choice.

Let's look at the definitions of each one.

Frequency   *Frequency* is a term that refers to the number of times one specific customer actually sees your ad. It may play 10 times, but if only one person sees it one time, your frequency is 1. We are all busy in our daily lives and are bombarded by messages all day long. We are not slaves to our radios, TVs, and newspapers, and ignore messages that don't address a pressing need at the time we hear or see them. That's why frequency is important. Every minute of every day someone needs your product or service and with frequency the message will be there when they do.

Use frequency if:

- You are trying to capture the same market as your competitor (McDonald's vs. Burger King). Think about the industries you see or hear about most often—car dealers, fast food, pet supplies, snack foods, and cleaning products. Highly competitive industries live or die with frequency.

- You want customers to order the product then and there. The Home Shopping Network (HSN), slicers and dicers, miracle mops, and other time-savers all use frequency.

- Customers must act within a certain time period. Weekend sales and limited-time offers are examples of use of frequency. Fear of loss is always more powerful than expectation of gain. "Act now! Don't miss out on this special offer!"

- There's not a lot of difference between you and your competitors. Because there's little difference between the Quarter Pounder and the Whopper, the message must be reinforced over and over.

Reach   *Reach* is a term that is often presented with frequency because they are first cousins.

Reach is the total number of households exposed to your message over a specific period of time. The best example of reach I can think of is the Super Bowl. The frequency of that particular ad placement is once a year and the reach is a good portion of the planet. Remember, when you run a newspaper ad it reaches a lot of people, but many of those people are not your customers and never will be. So reach is important to look at and must be used carefully.

Go for greater reach if:

- You are introducing a new product to a broad mass market and want as many people as possible to know about it. The greatest commercial ever made (according to *Advertising Age*) ran only one time—during the 1984 Super Bowl. It was the ad announcing the new Macintosh computer from Apple Computer.
- The message is so good customers will react immediately. Tickets to a hot concert would work here.
- The product is newsworthy (e.g., cancer cure), and will demand attention all by itself.

Impressions   Impressions refer to the total of all exposures of the ad to all people who see the ad. For example, a newspaper has 10,000 readers per day. Of those, 8,000 read the sports page on a regular basis. If you run an ad in the sports section every day for 30 days, that's 240,000 impressions (30 ads × 8,000 readers = 240,000). Are you beginning to see how advertising in the wrong medium can start to get expensive?

Ratings Points   Ratings points are measures of selected TV and radio audiences used to equalize in the customers' eyes how one program relates to another. Advertising pricing is then based on these numbers. More people voted on *American Idol* than voted in a recent general election. Since more people are watching *American Idol* than reruns of *Matlock*, the stations can charge a higher rate for more popular shows in prime time. Your job is to determine whether running your ads there will produce more return on your investment than the ads cost.

Media Objectives   Remember your sales objectives in Chapter 4? Here you will want to accomplish the same thing. You must have goals and objectives that you want your advertising to accomplish. If you don't have objectives, how are you going to evaluate whether your advertising was worth the expense?

If I were to write a media objective for my radio ads, it might look like this:

The ad should reach 75 percent of my primary target market an average of five times and at least 40 percent of my secondary market at least three times in the first 30 days. So, if I've defined my target market correctly, have a good offer, issue a strong call to action, and place my ads with the correct media, I should expect favorable results.

If your company were a large firm in a large city, your advertising agency would take care of all this for you as part of its services. But as a small business in a small town, you'll have to do it yourself because the town may not be big enough to have an ad agency. Let's look at how you do it.

How to Select the Right Media   Now that you have your goals and objectives of what you want advertising to accomplish, it's time to pick the right advertising media that will do the best job of reaching your target market with your message.

Advertising Possibilities   List and review as many advertising sources and possibilities as you can for reaching your target audience.

The cost of advertising is always going to be a concern, but don't worry about it at this point. We'll deal with it later on in the process. You want a list of as many ways to reach your target market as possible. For example, if I wanted to reach senior citizens, I might want to look at *Senior Golf Journal* and *Modern Maturity* magazine.

Many seniors own motor homes, so maybe *Motor Home* magazine would be a consideration. Seniors may be housebound, so the local edition of the *TV Guide* or the TV listings in the newspapers should be considered. As you weigh the various forms of advertising available, keep in mind the specifics and demographics of the market you are trying to reach. Do you want to reach all seniors, or just active seniors? Golfing seniors? Fishing seniors? The more you can narrow down the market, the easier it will be to find the right medium to reach good prospects.

List as many as you can, and don't limit your options. If you are currently in business, one of the best ways of finding out where your customers get their information is to ask them. Ask how they heard about you. Most people enjoy talking about themselves, so ask. They don't need to know you're doing research. Ask them fill out a Satisfaction Report Card. Warranty cards are another good source of information.

Radio and TV stations, magazines, and newspapers will each have demographic profiles of their readers, listeners, and viewers. Start by matching up the profiles of the various media with the profiles from the target market section of your marketing plan. The library will have listings and addresses of magazines that may be popular in your area. In Bozeman we have *Montana* magazine, and many Bozeman businesses advertise there.

Start with the biggest media first and narrow your choices as you go. I mentioned earlier that TV might be possible for a grand opening or big sale, but not day to day. With newspapers, the ads might be bigger for a huge sale but smaller for a name recognition run over a longer period. If you are doing outdoor advertising, your billboard company should provide you with pricing, availability, and location of available billboards, as well as the number of cars that will pass by.

Media Kit   Get a media kit from each potential medium and study it. A media kit will have all the necessary information about the readership of a newspaper or magazine, or the viewership or listenership of a TV or radio station. It should contain the demographics needed to match against your target market. If not, then ask your ad representative for the demographics.

Advertising Representative   Form a relationship with your advertising representative. These are the people who have the greatest influence as to where your ad may be placed or when it's aired. In small towns, the sales rep may also be the general manager at the radio or TV station. They can help you—make friends with them and let them know you appreciate their efforts.

Although most sales reps are paid on commission and are always trying to sell you more than you may need, they can often provide special deals and promotional offers that may cut costs.

Media Combination   Choose a combination of media with the right impact. Remember, your goal is to pick the least expensive advertising with the biggest bang for the buck. This refers to your whole package, not each individual part. Think cost per customer, not cost per thousand. Is the ad going to produce enough paying customers to pay for itself? If not, then it's not a good value.

A radio or newspaper ad may cost less, and reach a bigger segment of your target market for a longer time, than a one-time TV spot on prime time. Make your advertising pay.

Time Sensitivity   How time sensitive is your advertising?

If you are going to run a magazine ad, it may take three to six months before your ad will be seen by the customer. This is fine if you know in advance what you're going to run and for how long. Remember, magazines tend to hang around for weeks, months, even years in some doctors' offices. If you need a quick result, magazines are not your best bet even if the price is attractive. For short-time ads, use radio, newspapers, and TV. In most small towns it will be radio and newspapers.

Frequency and Exposure I defined frequency as the number of times a specific customer sees your ad. It has also been defined as the total number of times an ad is run in a specific medium. Let's go back to our comparison of time. Ads in the daily newspaper often end up on the bottom of the birdcage before the day is done. They are seen once and then the newspaper is in the trash. Your ad is gone.

Conversely, people tend to hang on to magazines that are devoted to their interests, and the ad stays around a little longer. Using this argument, a daily newspaper would require more frequency than a monthly magazine.

Be consistent in your advertising. An ad run three times in the same medium in the same place has a much better chance of being noticed than the same ad run only once or twice. Run it six to nine times and things can really get exciting. I can't stress this point enough. There is no instant gratification in marketing or advertising. It takes time to sow the seeds and reap the harvest. Put your message out there consistently and get it working.

If you invest in the stock market, there is always a chance the market will go down and you'll lose money. If the market goes up, you make money. Advertising and marketing are no different. They are investments. They are not too expensive. They aren't an expense at all (although it may seem that way when you sign the checks for them). Advertising, if done correctly, is an investment in your business and your future.

Many marketing books will tell you that running an ad too many times in the same place will bore people and the message loses impact.

I disagree with this thinking, because as a society we are not a stagnant pond; we are a whitewater rapids.

Think of your business like a parade slowly moving down Main Street. Your business is one of the floats in the parade. As you move down the block, people you are approaching are excited and anxious to see your float. As you pass by, they admire your float, take in your message, and then direct their attention to the next approaching float.

Would you change your float at this point? No, because in the next block there is an entirely new group of people anxiously awaiting your float, and the process repeats itself for the entire parade route. Your ad is constantly moving past new eyes day after day. It's the same to you each day, but to others it's always brand-new.

We are constantly on the move, and we dismiss many of the thousands of daily messages that bombard us. We move from place to place more than citizens of any other country on earth. Bozeman changes its entire population every 7 to 10 years, mostly because of the winters.

People were predicting that Montana's population would reach one million people by 1975. We're still at 800,000 for the state. Here is an experience of mine that might help put this idea in perspective.

Several years ago my wife and I attended an automobile show in San Diego. We both fell in love with the Mazda RX-7 but we could not recall seeing any of these cars in the San Diego area. However, we were amazed that on the drive home they seemed to be everywhere. We must have seen 15 to 20 on our drive back to our house. Why hadn't we seen these cars before? They were obviously there.

We decided that all cars, except for those in our immediate path, were blocked out of our minds as unimportant in our lives at that time. Once the possibility of actually buying one came into play, then those cars began to appear on our radar screen. How do you know how long an ad should run? If the ad is paying for itself and producing more profit than it costs, then why change? As long as your ad is producing profitable customers, let it run. I don't care how boring it is to you and your employees; it's new to a lot of people who will be seeing it for the first time and now suddenly have the need or desire for your product.

If it is not working after a reasonable period of time, it may be time for a new campaign. Campbell's soup has been using "M'm! M'm! Good!" for a long time and Budweiser has been the "King of Beers" for a very long time.

Demographic Numbers   How do I know the demographic numbers are right?

Radio, TV, and newspapers all fall under forms of industry self-regulation. They have taken it upon themselves to do their own policing and keep their industry clean. They use independent outside sources to conduct audits on various industries. That's not to say that they never embellish the numbers or present them in the best light possible.

For TV, it's the Arbitron Company and the ACNielsen Company that audit viewers and report who is watching what, and when. Magazines use the Business/Professional Advertising Association (BPAA). Newspapers use the Audit Bureau of Circulation (ABC).

What Should Advertising Cost?   Advertising costs are going to vary depending on where you live and the competition in your markets. Here are some things to consider as you look at the pricing in your backyard.

If the price of producing the ad is more than the actual cost of running the ad, something is wrong. Either you have a very expensive ad and aren't running it enough or you're running it in the wrong place.

Another way sales reps look at the cost of advertising is the good old "cost per 1,000 listeners/viewers" to a particular show or spot in the program lineup.

Your interest should be in the cost per customer of your advertising, not the cost per thousand. If I buy three spots for $10 each ($30) and that produces one customer who spends $20, what just happened? My advertising has suddenly become an expense, not an investment. You want to reach people, but if your advertising is producing nonpaying customers it's simply not reaching the right people.

Reduce Advertising Costs   When you open a new business, it seems like tons of money are going out of the business and nothing is coming in. And, since advertising takes time to have an effect, there is an initial perception that it's not working and there is the urge to either reduce advertising or stop advertising altogether.

So, can you reduce the cost of advertising until the buyers start coming? Yes, here are a couple of ways.

Co-Op Advertising   Companies will pick up part of your advertising tab if you include their logo and product information in the ads. For example, a paint store can run an ad featuring Benjamin Moore paints and the paint company will pay for a portion of the ad.

Caution: Submit the ad to the co-op company for approval first. If you don't use its logo and copy within its guidelines, the company will disqualify you for the funds. Also, be patient in waiting for the co-op money. It is almost always paid well after the ad has run. Sometimes weeks, even months may go by before the check arrives. One way to speed up payment is by offering to accept payment in the form of a discount on your next order.

Joint and Cross Promotions   Can you join forces with other companies and combine your advertising dollars? Video stores and pizza parlors, for example, could share advertising, or your paint company could team up with a drywall company.

Combining products will sometimes make both products stronger together than they were apart. Advertising them together is more economical than separately, and packaging products makes it more difficult for your competition to match your ads and for customers to do price comparisons.

Which Media Are Best for You? Next, I'll show you the different types of media available to you and examine the strengths and weaknesses of each.

Newspapers Newspapers are usually standard size and six columns wide (like the *New York Times* and the *Wall Street Journal*) or tabloid style (like the *National Enquirer*). They can be daily, biweekly, weekly, and in rare cases monthly.

Strengths of Newspapers

Speed: Ads can be produced and quickly placed in the newspaper. That way your ad can influence your customer immediately.

Local markets: Many small towns have some form of daily newspaper. They are one of the best ways to reach local and small markets. In larger cities there are often neighborhood newspapers that specialize in things like local movies playing, nightclub band schedules, and listings of local events. In many cases these local newspapers can be a wise use of your ad dollar.

Sections: You can pick the section of the paper where you'd like your ad to appear. For example, if you're a stockbroker your ad can be in the business section, a shoe store ad can be in the family section, and a grocery store in the food section. Be where your customers are! Keep in mind that placement like this might carry an extra fee, but if it's reaching your target market it might be worth it.

Budget: How big or small should your ad be? In most cases it will be the size your advertising budget can afford. If you are using pictures in your ad, make sure the ad is large enough to show the picture comfortably. If you can't afford a large ad, you have to decide how important the picture is. The great thing about newspapers is that they run ads in a variety of sizes that can fit most small business budgets.

Weaknesses of Newspapers

Short life: Sometimes the daily newspaper is on the bottom of the bird-cage by 10:00 AM. Even worse, if someone misses the paper one day, they miss your ad. Sometimes newspapers will hang around the office or the home for a few extra days, but the more time passes, the less effective the ad will be in producing customers.

Ad placement: Where's a good place for your ad to appear? How about next to the daily horoscope? Even people who don't believe in astrology often check it. But, even if you request location, you may not get it. Your ad can be lost among others on the page.

Demonstration: If your product's story is best told visually, newspapers have some real restrictions. Even photos require a good-sized ad to make them visible. TV might be a better buy here.

Newsprint: The quality of newspapers compared to magazines leaves a lot to be desired. The paper used is called newsprint. Your computer printer will produce 300 dots per inch (dpi) up to 1,200 dpi. Newspapers, however, are about 85 dpi—not the best way to produce high-quality photos of your computer circuitry. To produce that kind of quality on good paper, a copy of the daily newspaper would cost upwards of $25.

Dealing with Print Ads   I always advise people to have their ads created by professionals whenever possible. If you have good computer design software, you may want to create your own print ads. By good computer software, I'm not talking about Publisher or MS Word. Most print shops and newspapers will work with those programs reluctantly if they have to. But if you feel you have what it takes to create your own ads, here are a few things I do when I create an ad:

First, start with all the elements that must be in the ad. These include your logo, address, phone number, and any other items that contribute to name recognition. After I have those in place, I can then see how much space I have left for the message. I can enlarge or reduce these essential elements as needed as I work on the ad.

Next, I want to combine a strong attention-getting visual with a very brief, but powerful, message about the business. The purpose of the ad is not to make the sale; the purpose to the ad is to entice the customer to call, come by, or write to me. This is the call to action that will make the customer react to the ad. When that happens the sales process can begin.

I also want the copy to stay about one-eighth to three-eighths of an inch away from the edge of the ad. Why? Because I know my ad may be clumped in with a lot of other ads, and this little area of white space will help frame my ad and make it stand out from the others. Don't feel you have to fill every available inch of space with your message.

The same is true in brochures and business cards. These items aren't intended to make the sale. Their purpose is to alert customers to your business and educate them about a need they might not know they had.

Color?   If you can afford color, use it! If you can't afford it, do the best you can for now. Four-color ads get a much higher response than ads with no color at all. Adding a color or two is always better than just black and white. If you design your own ads and you are restricted to black, remember that gray is a shade of black. It's not another color. You can have a two-color look using one color (black) at 100 percent and mixing in a lesser percentage to create gray areas. Also, color may not be as costly as you think. At least consider pricing it when talking with your media rep.

Caution: Sometimes color will be used only in certain sections and on certain pages of the newspaper, so be careful of placement of your color ad. It would be better not to spend extra for color if it's not going to appear in a section or on a page where it will do the most good.

Size?   Make your ad as large as you can afford. Here is where advertising and marketing are an investment. If you go with the size ad you can afford now, you are safe; advertising is not a risk for you. But if you go with a larger ad, you should receive more calls and more business, and the ad pays for itself.

I would suggest testing an ad one step above what is comfortable for you financially. If it fails to produce enough additional customers to warrant the larger size, then you can cut back to the previous size. Larger ads are more noticeable on the page and allow more "call to action" items like coupons and special offers.

Newspaper Ad Position   To avoid being unhappy with the placement of your ad, make sure it will be in the correct section of the paper—economy, sports, editorial, and so on. In some cases you may be able to pay extra for special placement of your ad. The best places to be in the paper, best to worst, are:

1. *Page 2 or 3 of the news section.* This section is the principal reason people buy newspapers. The most important news will be reported in these pages. More readers are going to be exposed to your ad here than in any other section of the paper.

2. *The back page of any section (except classified ads).* Stories that begin on page 1 are often continued on the back page of the section. It's easier for the page layout designers to see how the flow of the stories will work.

3. *The first three pages of any section (except classifieds).* Again, papers are purchased because of the news they contain. Each section is designed by the editors to attract attention. And the great thing is your ad goes along for the ride.

4. *Pages 4 and after in the news section.* The news section is the first 10 pages or so in most papers. Bigger cities may have 18 to 20 pages in the front section, whereas smaller towns will have fewer. This is the best place to be unless your products are sports related or financial in nature.

Better Placement and Value   Many small businesses like to advertise in the weekly TV section. In San Diego, this section is filled with ads by construction people advertising home remodeling and room additions. They know the TV section stays around all week while the rest of the paper ends up in the trash. As a result there is more opportunity for the ad to be seen.

Regional Sections   In Montana, Billings is the largest city. The *Billings Gazette* is available in most towns and cities throughout the state. The *Gazette* often includes a regional section for Bozeman, Butte, Missoula, and other Montana municipalities. The regional sections may be available at a lower price but mostly contain club and organization news. These sections may not hold great interest for the majority of readers in your backyard.

You may not get the biggest bang for your buck in a regional section. Contact businesses that are currently in these sections and see what kind of responses they are experiencing. Also look at the types of businesses that are in this section. Who are they talking to?

Special Events Sections   Many newspapers have special events sections during the year focusing on car shows, boat shows, bridal fairs, home improvement, and so on. Before placing ads in these, see if it's possible to get a copy of the previous year's edition (most newspapers archive all their publications). If it's mostly ads, with some stock articles as filler between those ads, it's probably not a good investment of your advertising dollar.

Look at who advertised in the previous edition and ask them if they are planning on repeating their ads this year. Start your own archives of newspaper sections to see what advertising is working there.

Advertising Inserts   One of the best ways to advertise in the newspaper is with an advertising insert. Take an 8½ × 11 piece of paper, create an advertising piece, and have the newspaper include it as an insert delivered within the paper. Obviously there will be a charge for this service, but I think you will find that it's dramatically cheaper than an ad of the same size. In addition, it can be in color, or at least on colored paper. Black ink on bright yellow is the easiest-read color combination.

If you are selling a high-ticket item, you may want the flyer to go to only the more affluent parts of town. In that case, you can request that the paper include it in certain newspaper routes that correspond to your demographic profiles.

Key Your Ads   I told you earlier in the book that I would come back to this very important topic. In order for your advertising to be successful, you must have a way of measuring how well it's performing or not performing.

Are there ways to tell if specific ads are the reason paying customers are coming into your business? What you need is some kind of signal or alert that the customer has come to your business because of the ad. To accomplish this, you will need to somehow make the customers behave in a manner that will let you know where they saw the ad.

The most common key is a coupon. The customer has a need, sees your money-saving coupon, brings the coupon in, and voilà— buys the product. The customer came in because of the coupon. If you have coupons in lots of places, put a code of some kind on each coupon to show where it came from.

If it's in the *Daily Gazette* in the first week of June, your code might be DG1/6. If you have a lot of coupons in a lot of different places, the key code will let you know which medium is reaching your target audience and producing the most sales. If you don't receive coupons after a fair trial from a particular publication, consider changing the ad or going with a higher-producing publication.

Other keys: "Call and ask for Jim," "Ask about our special offer," or "Ask for our free report 'Ten Things You Should Know Before Buying a Widget.'"

Newspaper Ad Cost   Newspapers base their advertising pricing to you on their circulation numbers (how many people subscribe plus newsstand sales), the size of the ad, color, and any kind of special placement of your ad. Frequent advertisers get better pricing than once-in-awhile advertisers. Regular advertisers are the lifeblood of all newspapers. They need you just as much as you need them.

Before you sit down to make a deal, get their advertising rate sheets and examine them for all the standard ad packages they offer. For example, your ad might cost $100 for a one-time placement. If you sign a one-year contract to run the same size ad monthly, the price might drop to $80 per placement. Run it weekly and the price will probably come down even more. With the basic information on the rate sheets you have a starting point to work from.

What enhancements would make your ad better, and how much do you think the newspaper will give up to get your business? Suppose color is $150 for a one-time run and $120 per month for a 12-month contract. Do you think the paper might go for color for $100 per placement? The only way to know is to ask. They may say no. You might then say, "Okay, I really wanted color, so guess I'll have to think about this." They might make you a counteroffer.

If you have friends in noncompeting businesses, ask them what kind of deal they got from the newpaper. Do not under any circumstances mention to anyone any deals that might jeopardize your friends' financial arrangements with the paper. This is for your information only. If you go in and say, "My buddy got this deal, and I want it, too," it might cost you and him in the long run. What you want to come away with is a compromise that is fair to both parties. If your advertising works, you will want a long and prosperous relationship with your newspaper, and that is their end goal as well. Don't burn any bridges right off the bat, but go after the best deal you can. If it pencils out you will probably get it.

Final Thoughts on Newspapers   Not every small town or neighborhood has a great paper. But, even with their weaknesses, the newspaper is a great buy in most small markets and small towns for most companies. Keep in mind that cost is not the only consideration. Take the time to do a little research before committing to anything long-term. Make sure that whatever ad you run in this paper will reach your target market.

Magazines   Almost every kind of business has some kind of magazine devoted to it. It never ceases to amaze me, as I travel around giving my seminars and workshops, to see the wide variety of trade magazines that are available to small businesses. You can take almost any trade name or industry and add the word *Today* to it and you'll have a trade magazine.

Concrete Today, Mobile Homes Today, Bird Watching Today—the list goes on and on.

Magazines are classified by content (*New Yorker*), geography (*Montana* magazine), and whether they are business-to-business (*Inc.*), special interest (*Golf Digest*), or for general public consumption (*People*), in addition to the thousands of trade magazines for virtually every industry or trade you can think of.

Magazines are an anomaly in the print business. They are much like books. Unlike the newspaper that is likely to be filled with more bad news than good and to be read quickly and discarded, people look forward to each issue of their favorite magazine. They often set aside a special time to examine it in depth. Most of the time issues are kept in stacks or filed in closets, so your ad is also kept. If you leave someone alone in your living room, chances are they will pick up the nearest magazine to pass the time until you return.

The real power of the magazine is the demographics of the readership. The more specialized the market, the more powerful your ad becomes. If I am a hunter, I am going to subscribe to one or more hunting magazines. I am not only going to read the articles about hunters, but I am also going to examine the ads to see what products might be available that will enhance my hunting experience.

If your widget will help me, there is a very good chance that I will become your customer. I may buy the first time I see the ad, whereas other customers might not buy till the tenth time they see the ad; that's why it needs to be in the magazine over a period of time. Each month there is another reminder that you are still there to take care of customers and their needs whenever they are ready.

If your product has mass appeal like cars, *People* magazine might make sense if the reader fits your demographics. My hunting product might reach thousands of people, but if they are the wrong people, then I'm wasting my money. The product and the customer must match for a magazine ad to be a smart advertising purchase.

Here are some strengths and weaknesses of this amazing advertising tool.

Magazine Strengths

Long life: As I mentioned earlier, some magazines stay in doctors' offices and other venues for years. People save them, pass them around, and send in reader response cards. This allows your products or services to be exposed to other potential markets without additional cost.

Narrow target market: If you have a narrow or specialized target market, a magazine ad is an excellent way to reach those people. The more specialized your products are, the more powerful the magazine becomes. Readers with special interests are seeking out this type of information and will often pay more attention to the ads than a casual reader of *People* might. They are always looking for additional resources and related products that will enhance their emotional experience. If your ad pushes their hot buttons, a lot of business should be coming your way.

Versatility: Have you ever scratched off a spot in a magazine to sample a perfume fragrance? Ever returned a reader information card? Ever seen a foldout in a magazine? Special inks? Unusual shapes and sizes? Heavy paper? There are many things magazines can do to attract your customers that other media can't.

Credibility: Every company wants the *Good Housekeeping* Seal of Approval on its products. Some magazines have excellent reputations, and an ad transfers that reputation to your company in the eyes of some loyal readers. Readers sometimes assume that ads, like the magazine content and articles, are accepted rather than simply purchased.

Size and color: Magazines offer superb color (for a price) that other media can't touch. Many magazines are known for their photos and colorful reproductions of art and paintings. Over the years *National Geographic* has taken us to all the corners of the world with its high-quality photographs and vivid stories.

Magazine Weaknesses

Long lead time: It takes awhile to get your ad into the magazine. To advertise my books for Christmas, I need to have the ad copy in by the end of June. If I am going to run ads each month for a year, then I am looking 18 months into the future. In this fast moving world of computers and high-speed lifestyles, that's a very long time.

High cost: Many national magazines are price prohibitive. The cost of a national ad in *People* can exceed $100,000 per page. If that's your market and if the ad produces more customers than it costs, then it's not expensive. But there is an alternative possibility.

Many national magazines produce regional issues, and those rates, though still high, are more reasonable for small business. *TV Guide* is a good example of a magazine that offers regional advertising.

Limited space: Magazine editors don't want the ads to overpower the content of the magazine (except in the case of *People* special issues, where the ad pages often outnumber the content 2 to 1). It's easy for your ad to be lost in popular magazines because they are crowded. Choose your magazine wisely.

Low frequency: Monthly magazines are 12 issues per year. You may need additional advertising in other places to reinforce your magazine advertising. If you need to reach more people more often, magazines might not be the best place for you. But if your competitors are there month in and month out, there must be a reason. Just remember advertising must pay for itself.

Magazine Ad Placement   The best places to put your ad in a magazine, best to worst, are:

1. *The inside front cover.* Sometimes this is where the table of contents is located, so being across from that is a great placement.

2. *The back cover.* Not everyone puts a magazine down face up. There is at least a 50 percent chance you will get as much exposure on the back cover as the front cover.

3. *The first few pages of the magazine.* Customers may pick your magazine up at a newsstand and start thumbing through it. The first few pages are designed to draw readers in and keep them there. This is a competitive area, as there might be a limited number of ad pages before the meat of the magazine begins.

4. *Directly across from the cover story or the feature story.* Many magazines use ads as buffers between stories, and it's a great way to

expose the ads to their readers. Remember that magazines want to give you every ad opportunity they can.

5. *The inside back cover.* Sometimes people start at the back of the magazine and work forward. I know it doesn't seem to make much sense, but there are people—like me—who do that.

There are only three other places your ad can be: the first 25 percent of the magazine, the next 50 percent of the magazine, or the last 25 percent of the magazine.

These locations may vary in desirability from magazine to magazine, so use the list as a guide, not an absolute.

One way to find out what's successful in magazines is to look at back issues. If the same companies keep showing up in the same spot month after month, you know their advertising must be working.

Some Final Thoughts on Magazines   If you can afford magazine advertising, especially in color, it can be very rewarding for your business. It stays around a long time as opposed to other media and has the power to be the most professional and eye-catching presentation. If your business has a narrow interest, this may be the smartest way to go.

Radio   Radio has three advertising categories: local, spot, and network.

Most advertisers in small towns and small markets use local ads. They are usually 30- or 60-second commercials played on a rotating schedule or at specifically selected times. These would be ads for Joe's Shoe Store's big semiannual sale or the specials at the local hardware store.

Spot ads are sold to national advertisers to play in local markets. If you've ever seen an ad for a political candidate, you've seen an example of this form of advertising. These ads are sold to play in states close to the primary elections of each state. They may vary slightly based on the culture of the state or area. Another example would be a furniture company that has stores in many states. It would buy ads to play in each market where a store exists.

Network ads will reach all stations in the national network. For example, stand-up comedian Jeff Foxworthy has a nationally syndicated music show that reaches many cities. If you are after the conservative or liberal market, there are Rush Limbaugh or Ed Schultz. For sports, try ESPN radio. For business, there is the *Start-Up Nation* national radio show.

As with any other medium, it all boils down to your target market. Who's listening and why?

Radio Strengths

Reach and influence: Radio reaches a lot of people quickly, and it reaches a larger audience than any other medium. Homes often have multiple radios. Car radios, portable radios, and radios in the workplace expose your business to countless thousands every day. Many businesses will have the radio on for atmosphere. The Gap may have rock music blaring, while Nordstrom might have easy listening in the background.

Production costs: Radio commercials are often less expensive to create than TV commercials. You can create a word picture on radio of something that would be cost prohibitive to produce for TV.

Cost per thousand: Radio advertising is priced at cost per thousand listeners. It's one of the lowest cost-per-thousand rates available. Keep in mind that numbers are not the end all, be all of advertising. They must be the right numbers—your customers. Later in the book I will cover the importance of cost per customer.

Radio can be tricky in larger markets because of the cost per thousand policies. WLS in Chicago, for example, reaches not only all of Chicago, but also half of Wisconsin and Illinois. Is it worth it for you to purchase an audience of this size? Your ads might produce enough customers to make it worthwhile, but you are paying to reach a lot of noncustomers who may never visit your business.

Formats: Radio station formats include talk, rock, new age, rap, country, classical, and contemporary, to name just a few. Each station has its own distinctive audience, and some are not talking to your specific market. Your advertising sales rep should be able to help you match your target market to the right station or programming. If your business can profit from radio, it's a very economical buy in most markets (but be careful in larger cities).

Anything you can imagine: Several years ago comedy ad guru Stan Freberg made a commercial touting the power of your imagination in the use of radio. In the commercial, Lake Michigan had been drained and filled with hot chocolate and a plane towing a giant marshmallow was flying over to drop it. Can you picture this in your mind? With today's computer enhancements this would be easy to create on TV, but the production costs could be astronomical. On radio just paint a word picture and you're done.

Radio Weaknesses

Short shelf life: Unlike magazines, once the commercial airs it's gone forever. It's not around to refer to later. You either heard it or you didn't. For that reason radio requires lots of spots on different stations to reach the majority of the listeners.

Visuals: If your customer needs to see your product to appreciate it, then radio is very limited. I listed appealing to the imagination as a radio strength, but would you have been able to paint a word picture of the hula hoop on radio? It wouldn't have been impossible, but TV would tell the story much better. You might have used radio to direct the customer to a product demonstration, but for the most part radio would have been a waste of money promoting that phenomenal toy.

Listener loyalty: Radio is a very competitive market. In Bozeman we have 14 radio stations for all of the Gallatin Valley. That's about 80,000 listeners at this writing. Most of these listeners are very loyal to their stations, so it may be necessary to advertise on several stations instead of just one or two to reach your target market.

Broad range of listeners: There are several types of stations that cross demographic lines. All ages listen to country as well as rock and roll. However, the classical music station might not have as much diversification. If you're selling to business owners, for example, unless you are advertising on a show that caters just to them, all nonbusiness listeners will largely ignore your message. Knowing the range of your market is critical to successful radio.

Background: Many listeners have the radio on at work at a low volume for background music and never consciously hear your commercial. This is not all bad, though, because your subconscious mind remembers everything it hears or sees. So your commercials are cataloged and may rise to the surface when the time and need are there. Have there been times when you recognized a company name but weren't sure where you had seen or heard it?

Message Content A radio message usually has three major components:

1. An *attention-getting introduction*. Distinctive music, sound effects, or jingles can accomplish this. If you can't get listeners' attention at the very beginning of the ad, the impact will be greatly reduced.

2. *The main message*. The commercial should create interest in the product or service and, most important, the benefits of that product or service.

3. A *call to action*. A clear and compelling closing message requires listeners to act, and act now, or they are going to miss out: "Come down today!" "Buy now!"

Check 'Em Out Do a little homework. Get the listings of radio stations in your area and start listening to them. Listen to a different station each day. You may not care for the programming choices of some stations, but your customers just might. It might be the type of music or the program content, but get in touch with the types of entertainment that are available to your customers.

Pay particular attention to who is advertising on what station. Who are they speaking to? Does the tone of the commercial fit the station? You probably won't find a commercial for the upcoming symphony season on the rap station.

Target Market Match   When choosing a station, you will need to match your target market to the station. Here are some ways to do it:

From your target market profile, when is your target market most likely to be listening? Do they go to work early? Do they work nights? Weekends? This information is very important in helping your sales rep match your market to the right show or station. The more you can tell the rep about your customers, the more the rep will be able to help you get the most bang for your advertising buck.

Match your product to the station's programming—for example, Cadillacs and investment shows, lawn mowers and gardening shows, fishing equipment and outdoor shows. Think of specialized radio shows and magazines of the airwaves. Just like with magazines, a fishing enthusiast is going to pay attention to the fishing or hunting show. And, if he hears about a sale on fishing equipment at a local store he will probably go check it out after the show. The host of the show can help the advertiser by mentioning the sale products during the show. For example, the host might talk about a type of lure he has found effective for catching trout, knowing that the advertiser carries that type of lure.

Radio Ad Placement   Creating a quality radio ad is just the beginning. The next step is placing your ad in the most effective position. Just like the newspaper and magazines, there are certain places you want to be on radio.

The best placements for radio ads (best to worst) are:

1. *Morning and evening drive time*. On the way to and from work, you have a captive audience sitting in traffic with the radio as a diversion.

2. *Weekend mornings*. People sit down with a cup of coffee and the newspaper, and flip on the radio to catch up on the weather, news, and so on.

3. *Work hours for certain kinds of stations*. Jazz, easy listening, and classical stations are used as background music in many businesses. Although this may not seem to be the ideal place to put your ads, they still receive exposure in a lot of retail establishments.

4. *Specialty shows*. Tie your product into a theme show. For instance, tie your camping equipment to an outdoor show or your car detailing business to a car show.

Guidelines for Radio   Here are four pointers to keep in mind when using radio.

1. Running several commercials per day over a period of weeks is better than spacing them out over a period of months. Years ago I played guitar in a band. I still play, but if I don't do it regularly I get rusty. The same thing happens with advertising. Keep your advertising in front of customers on a regular basis so it stays in the forefront of their minds and keeps them thinking about your products.

2. If you're in a group of commercials at the top of the hour, ask to be the first commercial in the chain. Listeners will still be focused on the show and you can keep their attention.

3. Ask to have your commercials placed in the middle of the show rather than the beginning or the end. Once the program ends, the listener may turn off the radio and go do something else. I host two local radio shows and have had many listeners tell me that after my show they do exactly that.

4. You might want to ask an announcer who is well respected in your community to read your commercial live. This practice continues the tone of the program and is more likely to keep the listeners' attention.

Final Thoughts on Radio   All things considered, for the small or new business, radio is the best value available for reaching large numbers of customers quickly, easily, and inexpensively. Radio spots can be produced and on the air in a matter of hours as opposed to days and sometimes months for other media.

Television   Most small towns don't have local television stations. However, I'm going to cover this area because the time may come when your business reaches a size that you'll want to advertise on one of the TV stations that reach your community. And the television industry is the most powerful means of reaching mass numbers of customers quickly.

The thing to remember about television is that your customers are looking at thousands of moving images per hour. You still have the same challenge—capture their interest and burn the image of your product into their psyches. What is the major topic of conversation the day after the Super Bowl? The commercials. Which was best? Entire shows are devoted to the evaluation of these commercial messages.

Television has gone through several transitions. For years, the big three television networks had a lock on all TV viewers. ABC, NBC, and CBS were the only entertainment options in the nation and did virtually all of the advertising. In the late 1960s cable started to emerge and siphon off some of the network viewers.

Cable movie channels began to offer what every TV viewer dreamed of: an uninterrupted show with no commercials. HBO, Cinemax, and Showtime flourished, winning many awards for their innovative productions.

Then came specialty channels that carried advertising: ESPN, the Weather Channel, the Discovery Channel, Home Shopping Network, the Sci Fi Channel, Comedy Central, and yes, even the Golf Channel, among others. With cable the business advertiser could now pick and choose which channels to be on and when.

Package deals became available, and the small business advertiser could be on several channels each day for less than a single spot on a network prime-time show. For the first time, television advertising was finally available to Main Street, USA.

In radio, as I mentioned, people tend to stay with one station most of the time. In TV people "channel surf" through the selections until they find something that interests them. Cell phones are miniature TV receivers that can send and receive snapshots, video clips, and TV shows.

High-definition TV and YouTube are the order of the day: better picture, better sound, and the Internet right on your TV screen. What else is coming in the future? Anything the mind can think of.

One day in the not-too-distant future you will be watching a TV show, see someone in a suit or dress you like, click on it, and after the show go to a cyberstore on your TV where you will get the price and sizes. You will then be able to order the article right off the TV with a credit card. Men would love to shop this way, but I think the jury's still out on the women.

Like any other medium we've discussed, TV has its good points and bad points. Here are some things to consider before committing to television advertising.

Strengths of TV

Broad reach: The biggest strength of TV is that it reaches almost everyone. Not everyone reads the newspaper or magazines, but almost everyone watches TV some portion of every day, either for entertainment, news, or just relaxation. TV can reach and influence better than any other advertising medium. If a picture truly is worth a thousand words, then TV can tell your picture story.

It's visual: If your product requires some kind of demonstration or instruction, TV is your medium. Could magazines and newspapers have sold the hula hoop as well as TV did?

It uses both sight and sound: Radio is hearing, while newspapers and magazines are seeing. TV combines not only sight and sound but also, depending on your imagination, taste and smell.

Ever see a food ad and your mouth starts watering? You can almost smell the hot rolls or pizza.

Using actors and other celebrities: In national ads, people like Gene Hackman, Ed McMahon, and others make a good living as spokespersons for certain products. Advertisers feel that we perceive these people as honest and sincere and we'll be more comfortable buying the product from them. "Go into the store and tell them Ed sent you." In a small town you probably aren't going to get Gene Hackman or Brad Pitt to do the commercials for your store or service, but there are local folks who have celebrity status on a local level.

Radio disc jockeys are the best known, and if they are credible, use them if you can. You may have high-profile customers who might agree to be in your ads. Nothing is more powerful than a testimonial from someone people know.

Brand identity: If you are trying to establish your brand name, logo, or package design, TV is very powerful. Viewers can see the product in use and see the colors of the package. Showing the packaging in living color on the screen gives the mind a complete picture to work with.

When customers then see the package on the store shelf, it's much like seeing an old friend. "I recognize you!" Our local Linens 'n Things store has an "As Seen on TV" section of products—everything from the tap light to the pocket fisherman.

Weaknesses of TV

Cost: Even in small markets, TV can be expensive initially. But over time, if it's reaching the right market, it can be very effective and will pay for itself like advertising should.

Production costs, time, locations, ideas, and reshoots can all add to the expense. But when the commercial is finally done, it can be played for months—even years—for only the spot costs.

One way small business owners save money on TV advertising is to use national ads that have already been made at corporate expense and add your name (called a tag or tagline) and address at the end of the commercial. If you're a paint store, maybe Dutch Boy has taped commercials you can use, and will pick up part of the cost as co-op advertising. Ask your sales rep for money-saving suggestions that have been used with other advertisers. Remember they want you to be a longtime advertiser. It's in their best interest to help you.

Here today and gone today: Like radio, once the message is delivered on television, it's gone. Newspapers and magazines keep your ad around awhile, but your TV commercial is gone and the next message is on the way. However, with VCRs and TiVo, it can be seen again when the tape is replayed and can be passed along to others.

Reinforce your message with repetition: Due to the thousands of messages our brains receive every day, TV spots must be seen often to be effective. Chances are you have watched a *CSI* or *Law & Order* marathon over a holiday weekend. Did you see the same commercials over and over again? Chances are very good that you did—sometimes to the point you were sick of them. This is the exception, not the rule. Not everyone sits down for six to eight hours of nonstop TV watching. People come and go. Running the commercial hour after hour is the most effective way to reach the most sets of eyes and ears.

What Are the Components of Successful TV Commercials?   Have you ever seen an ad in a magazine that looked just like a scene from the TV ad for the same product? A good test of a TV ad is: Could you take a single frame from your TV ad and make a magazine ad from it? If you can, then the image is successfully telling the story.

All good movies have a beginning, a middle, and an end. It's the same with TV. Get the viewer's attention, tell the story, reaffirm the message, and end with a strong "call to action" finish. TV tells a story that draws viewers in and makes them part of the action. They see themselves using the product, feeling good about themselves, improving their appearance, or having the best lawn in the neighborhood. These are 30- to 60-second movies that can influence and direct just as effectively as their 90-minute big brother productions can.

Placing TV Advertising   Chances are you will be placing your own TV ads, so here are some things to think about. This can be a dangerous activity for your business. It isn't that TV is more difficult than print or radio; the problem is the cost of a mistake. One mistake—your message in the wrong place or wrong target market—and changes can be as expensive as starting from scratch.

There is no question that TV can be very profitable to the small business owner when used correctly. *Correctly* is the key word here. The first question to ask is, "Are my competitors here?" If they are, then that might be a good sign that the shows or times you have chosen have a good chance of success. However, don't base an expense of this size on that one factor.

Check, double-check, and triple-check that your target market is really going to be watching when you run your spots. Study and restudy your customer demographics to make absolutely sure they line up with the station or show you have chosen. Have a strong key in the ad that will let you know that the ad is working along with a powerful call to action that will be hard for the customer to resist.

Some Final Thoughts on TV   The most economical form of TV advertising is spot advertising. Local spots in your area are available for the Super Bowl—not at hundreds of thousands of dollars for each minute but at local pricing based on your local station's viewership. The Super Bowl in your local market will be higher in price than you would pay for a normal local ad, but it may still be a bargain for you if enough people in your local area are watching.

Keep in contact with your local sales rep for upcoming special programming that might attract your target market. Local sports are a great way to get some exposure for your business. Don't wait until your local team is ready for the championship game to buy your spots. Make a deal at the beginning of the season that if the team reaches the finals and TV coverage is planned, you will commit to a certain number of spots. That way you'll be locked in at a favorable price and your competitors will be locked out.

Like radio, TV works best when you run ads several times over a period of weeks instead of months. Try to run commercials in the middle of the show rather than at the end of one show and the beginning of another. There is usually a teaser at the halfway point in a show to encourage us to stay and see the second part of the show.

If you are going to run several spots in the same evening or during the same show, have two or three variations of the same commercial ready so the audience won't get bored seeing the same message over and over. Due to production expenses this may not always be possible, but using the same sets and same people and shooting all versions at once can save you some money over making three different commercials over time.

If you can afford TV ads in your market and you can make good spots that produce results, then use that medium. Keep in mind that there is a lot of testing in finding the right message and the right way to present that message. Give TV a fair chance. Advertising takes time to work, no matter what vehicle you are using. But nothing I can think of is more powerful than TV for reaching large numbers of customers and building name recognition fast.

Yellow Pages   The most used way to find a service or business on a local level in the United States is by far the yellow pages. For some unknown reason, the term *yellow pages* was never copyrighted by anyone, so you see it used by all sorts of local telephone directories.

"Let your fingers do the walking" is a very powerful slogan that says it all. If you think you don't use the yellow pages that much, put the directory in the basement for a month and see how many times you reach for it. If you are in a service business such as carpet cleaning, or are a plumber, carpenter, contractor, or electrician, you'll probably get a lot of calls from the yellow pages.

Let's talk about the right way and wrong way to use the yellow pages; then we'll explore the strengths and weaknesses. When you sit down with your yellow pages rep, he or she is going to try to convince you to buy the largest ad possible. There's nothing wrong with that; it's what they are paid to do. But is it the right decision for you? Here's what to look for.

Start by letting others do the testing, make the mistakes, and spend the money for you. By that I mean look in past yellow pages to see who is there, where they are in the directory, and how big their ads are. If you see the same companies with the same ads year after year, then something must be working. If the size of the ad increases or decreases, that should tell you something, too.

Check the local library for its copies of yellow pages from other areas. Look for towns comparable to yours. If you are in a small community, then look at towns in regional areas similar to yours. Are you in a tourist area, agricultural area, rural area, or metropolitan area?

If you are a current yellow pages advertiser, should you go with a bigger ad? Only if you are sure that the larger ad will produce enough additional customers to justify the higher cost. If you have good reason to believe it will, then give it a shot. But remembering the rule that advertising must pay for itself, the larger ad may turn out to be an expense rather than an investment. In a big city the larger ad would probably pull enough additional customers, but in a town with a smaller customer base you should be more careful. I'm not saying don't go for a bigger ad; just make sure the population and customer base pencil out.

Here are the strengths and weaknesses of the yellow pages:

Yellow Pages Strengths

Buyers: By the time people get to the yellow pages, they are already sold; they are looking for the place to buy.

Credibility: Most fly-by-night companies don't go to the time and expense of a yellow pages ad. If a company has a yellow pages ad, there is a perception that company is probably honest and capable.

Classifications: If your business wears many hats, you can advertise under several headings. For example, a company that sells copier machines may also sell office furniture and would want to be under both listings to increase its customer base.

Free copy: Every person and business in your selling area that has a phone gets a free copy of your ad. Yellow pages are used by 89.9 percent of all adults. They give you total market coverage.

Twenty-four hours a day: It's ready to go, and if you're a 24-hour business, customers are ready to buy.

Cost: The cost per thousand is relatively low compared to other media. (Remember to track cost per customer in your ad.)

Extends the reach of other media: "See our ad in the Yellow Pages under widgets."

Yellow Pages Weaknesses

Naked to the world: I turn to your yellow pages ad and there you are— with *all* of your competitors. There is a chance I might call a company with a bigger ad, or one that says it provides the specific service I need.

Long lead time: You need to have your ad ready almost six months before the new phone book comes out.

No updates: Change of address, new phone, new services, and discontinued services? Sorry, no update until the new phone book comes out.

Coupons: I was working with a video company in San Diego at the beginning of the video store boom in the early 1980s. We made the major mistake of putting a two-for-one movie rental coupon, with no expiration date, in our yellow pages ad, good at any of the 15 stores we had at that time. During the early days of video rental, the average one-night rental price was $5.

People got coupons out of phone booths, offices, and everywhere else; no phone book in the city was safe. For almost 18 months we gave away thousands of dollars' worth of free movie rentals. It was a very painful lesson. Before you start to feel too sorry for us, though, we did go on to build 42 stores in San Diego and eventually sold the chain to Blockbuster Video for $12.5 million.

Final Word on the Yellow Pages   The consensus here is clear. If you can afford to be in the yellow pages, do it. When I first opened my marketing business in 1985, the profit from my first call paid for my yellow pages ad for the year. However, I placed a larger ad in a regional yellow pages and never received a single call from that ad. I'm not saying don't advertise in regional yellow pages, but you may want to ask owners of similar businesses how their ads are doing.

When in doubt, do what I did: Test an ad and find out. If it works, next time buy a larger ad. Two good yellow pages resources to help you design and buy ads that work are *Advertising in the Yellow Pages*, by W. F. Wagner (Harvest Press, 1986), and *Getting the Most from Your Yellow Pages Advertising*, by Barry Maher (Barry Maher & Associates, 2006).

The last bit of sage advice pertains to the next advertising medium I'll cover, which is the Internet. If you have a display ad in the yellow pages, add this to it: "For unadvertised specials and discounts, visit our web site at www.yourcompany.com."

The reason for this is to get customers out of the yellow pages and away from all your competitors lined up next to you. Move them to your web site, where you can show them why they should be doing business with you.

Internet

There is no question the Internet has changed all our lives. In a matter of moments you can be educated about the most obscure topics and events. Even if you have never been online, the actions of those who have similar demographics to yours have made it easier for you to purchase almost anything.

Four thousand Stanford University students were asked to select their favorite Internet activities from a list of 17 categories. As you might expect, e-mail was the number one, used by over 90 percent of the respondents. Thirty-three percent use the Web for entertainment and games, while another 25 percent visit chat rooms. (Interesting enough, the study revealed that after the age of 25, chat room visits drop substantially.) Other uses include buying stocks, auctions, and online banking by another 25 percent.

The most important finding revealed the reasons certain economic and demographic groups used the Internet. You might think the reasons would be tied to income, race, or gender. But the common denominator across all groups is education. A college education will add 40 percentage points to Internet usage over the lowest educational groups in the study.

A research study at Ball State University's Center for Media Design recorded the usage of 350 Internet users. Sixty percent of users spent more than two hours on the Web every day either at home or at work.

The researchers also found that those users who were considered "Web dominate" (i.e., those who used the Web over all other sources of information) spent on average over $5,000 more per year on retail goods and services than those who were considered "TV dominate."

During morning drive time, TV has a reach of 41 percent, but when it's combined with the Internet it jumps to 62 percent. Newspapers have a reach of 17 percent, but add the Internet and you are looking at 44 percent. At night when TV, newspapers, and the Web are combined, the reach goes from 39 percent to 75 percent.

The Internet is also reaching rural areas. Fifty-five percent of U.S. farms have Internet access. Eighty percent of farms with incomes in excess of $250,000 are Internet connected. More and more farmers and ranchers are turning to the Internet for all sorts of information about agricultural topics. Wives who only a few years ago were shopping out of Sears catalogs are now making their selections from a host of online retailers, both local and national.

According to the Online Publishers Association, the Internet is either #1 or #2 behind TV during almost any part of the day. Between the hours of 8:00 and 11:00 in the morning, the Internet has surpassed radio in popularity. The Internet is busiest between the hours of 2:00 and 5:00 in the afternoon. During this time almost 40 percent of all users are online.

So What?   What do these numbers and percentages mean to you and your customers? What they show is that people are being directed from one medium to another. More than that, they are being directed from a medium with time and space constraints to a medium with virtually no constraints. A web site can have instant updates, text, four-color presentation, multimedia, music, voice, multilingual capability, education, and almost unlimited pages. What other medium can do all that?

Can you find a national TV commercial that doesn't have a web site in it somewhere? How about ads in newspapers? Radio? Direct mail? Company name, phone, address, and web site are all there. Over the past 10 years advertising has spent countless billions showing us that the best source of information is the Internet. Dollar for dollar, there is no cheaper way of reaching the masses than online.

How Will Customers Find Your Site?   Having a web site is just the beginning. You need traffic to make your site effective. There are literally billions of sites on the Internet, so how can your site rise to the top where customers will see you?

You also need to attract the right visitors to your site. Even if a web site gets millions of visitors, it's meaningless unless they are visitors who become customers. Once again, this is why identifying your target market correctly is vital to your success.

Search Engines   The most popular way for someone to find something on the Internet is to go to a search engine. Type in a word (such as *spider*), and the search engine will find all the sites that deal with spiders for you. Then you can scroll through the pages and pick a site by clicking on it. A point to remember when searching: If you enter the word "Coffee" with a capital C, the search engine will return only pages that have Coffee with a capital C. If you enter the word "coffee," the search engine will return all instances of both "coffee" and "Coffee."

Normally your Internet service provider (ISP) will offer to submit your site to search engines. The ISP has the knowledge and is familiar with the procedures. You can submit your site to some search engines yourself. One place you should definitely submit your site to is the Open Directory Project at www.dmoz.org. Dmoz (from directory .mozilla.org, its original domain name) is a directory where live human beings review your site and decide on the best category to place it in. Most of the major search engines get their information from dmoz.

If you don't submit your site to search engines yourself or have your ISP do so, all is not lost. Every six weeks or so, the entire Internet is "crawled" by electronic robots sent from search engines to catalog the Internet. They visit each site, look at each page, and follow any links within or out of the site. If they find any site that links to you, then they will crawl your site, too, and you will be cataloged to that search engine.

One of the easiest ways to make this happen is to join your local chamber of commerce, and have them place a link to your site from theirs. If you have any suppliers that might list web sites of local dealers, this will accomplish the same thing. Do you want to know if you are in a search engine now? Simply type your address (www.yourcompany.com) into the search engine box, and if you come up, you are in there somewhere.

There are six major search engines: Google, MSN, Ask.com, AltaVista, Infoseek, and HotBot. There is also one other, the most popular, called Yahoo! Yahoo! is a special case because it's not a search engine at all. It's an index of sites in categories that is compiled and updated daily by editors and commonly referred to as a directory.

Search Engine Optimization　Search engine optimization (SEO) is the process of constructing your web site to be search engine friendly. Think of search engines as giant electronic yellow pages, out of control. In the traditional yellow pages, companies are placed in categories. All the carpet stores are together, shoe stores, and so on. The search engine structure of the Internet is not so refined.

Search engines process, and place, web site information according to each search engine's particular criteria. As a result, each search engine looks at your site differently, and where you rank in each may vary widely. You might be number one in one search engine and number 1,500 in another. So is there a way to increase the odds of search engines ranking your site more favorably? The answer, fortunately, is yes.

Relevance and Keywords　Let's go back to the traditional yellow pages for a moment. Remember that companies are placed in categories, so a shoe store would not be in the pet supplies category no matter how badly the owner might like to be there. The reason is the company and the category are not *relevant* to each other. And therein lies the secret to search engine optimization.

Because of the vast numbers of web sites, search engines don't offer a selection of categories. Instead, they ask you, the searcher, to use *keywords* to tell the search engine what you are looking for. The search engine subscribes to various directories, which are in categories, and returns the most relevant sites to you based on the keywords you selected.

The more relevant the web site is to the search terms, or keywords, the more the search engine likes it and will give it a higher ranking. If you are looking for pet supplies and a shoe store ad shows up on the page, that might diminish your confidence in that search engine. Obviously the search engine doesn't want that to happen, so a site with both pet supplies and shoes will not achieve as high a ranking as one that is strictly for pet supplies, because it's not as relevant.

At this point you have two terms that will make your site successful: keywords and relevance. The next step is to start thinking like your customers. Again, identification of your target market is critical to your online success. What keywords are they going to type into the search engine to find you? This may not be as simple as you imagine.

I teach business classes, so you might think those would be good keywords to use for customers to find me. However, when I explored those words I found most searches were people looking for airline business class flights. So even though the words were apropos to me, most searches would not have matched up to me. Business training would be a much better choice.

You are probably asking how I researched those keywords. Here are two sites I recommend for this task. One is the Overture Keyword Suggestion Tool from Yahoo! at http://inventory.overture .com/d/searchinventory/suggestion/. From Google try https:// adwords.google.com/select/KeywordToolExternal. There are many such tools available. Just do a search for "keyword suggestion tools" and several will pop up.

Keyword Placement After you have matched up your keywords with your target market, the next order of business is placing the keywords where search engines can not only find them, but also assign high relevance to them.

Here are the elements of a web site that search engines are going to look at to evaluate your relevance to its criteria.

- *Your domain name*. As much as I would have liked to call my site tomegelhoff.com, no one is going to search for that. So using keywords, I named the site smalltownmarketing.com, because that is exactly what my customers are searching for. If you already have an existing web site, don't worry about changing the domain name at this point. You might undo any positive rankings you already have. But if you are in the process of creating your name, keep search terms in mind when you consider your new name. If the name you want is not available, try adding a geographic keyword to it. For example, realestate.com is not available, but realestatedesmoines.com might be. Be creative in your thinking on domain name.

- *Your page title.* Your page title appears in the blue bar at the very top of your screen. This is the biggest mistake I see companies make. The title says "Home Page" and/or "Microsoft Internet Explorer" or some other nondescriptive term. My home page title is "small town marketing—How To Advertise, Market and Promote Your Business Or Service In A Small Town by Small Business Expert Tom Egelhoff." How many keywords are in that title that business owners are likely to type in as search terms? At least eight.

- *Your page headings.* There are three main headings used in the hypertext markup language (HTML) that the Internet uses. They are called H1, H2, and H3. H1 is the biggest and H3 is the smallest. The bigger the header, the more importance the search engines assign to it and its content. So this is an important place to have keywords. Use them in headlines and subheads in articles to improve the relevance of your pages.

- *Your page description.* When someone does a search, there is usually a description that appears with each site that comes up in the search. Here is another place that keywords play a major role, not only in raising your rank, but also telling customers why they should click on your site. If you don't use this feature, the search engine will substitute the first few lines of text on the page, and that may not be the message you want to send to customers. Take a little extra time and write a keyword-rich description.

- *Hyperlinks*. Hyperlinks are the lines of text that are usually underlined, and you click on them to go to another page or site. In most cases you will see something like: "For more information on prime real estate in Seattle, Washington, <u>Click Here</u>." So what's the problem with that? How many keywords are in the description? "Prime real estate" and "Seattle, Washington." Although the search engine gives weight to those terms, it would give them more relevance if the entire sentence was a link—the reason being that the purpose of a link is to provide more information relevant to the search terms. Your link should say: "For more information on prime real estate in Seattle, Washington, Click Here."

- *Additional pages for specific keywords*. When you think of a web site with many pages, think of each page as a separate individual web site all by itself. Each page on your web site contains all of the elements I've covered so far. Not every visitor will enter your site from your home page. They might find your article with the page title "How to Change Your Own Oil," rather than your home page of www.doityourselfcarcare.com. If you have lots of products or you have several target markets, create a page that talks to each one.

- *Graphics*. Pictures and graphic elements are invisible to search engines. The search engines catalog the site's text code, and graphics are irrelevant. Now there is a way to make photos and graphics visible to search engines. For that you will use a tool called the alt attribute to specify alternate text. Alt text is commonly used to describe things on the Internet for vision-impaired users. Use it to describe pictures of your products and services; just make sure keywords are included in the descriptions.

For more information on making your site more search engine friendly, see www.highrankings.com.

Tracking Results   The Internet also has some of the best tracking and marketing tools available anywhere. When customers go to a web site, their actions and movements can be tracked by placing a small piece of computer code on the page. As each page is accessed, the code on that page keeps track of what the customer is doing. One site that has both free and modestly priced tracking features is at www.websitetrafficreport.com. A free service is available through Google Analytics at www.google.com/analytics/.

What to Look For   Here are some things you'll want your tracking program to tell you about your visitors. What pages did they visit? How long did they stay on each page, and how long did they stay on the site? Did they make a purchase? Did they fill out an order but then leave without buying? Did they download a report? What entry page did they use to come into your site? Only about 20 percent of my Web traffic comes through my home page.

The actions of the visitors will tell the webmaster what changes, if any, to make on the site to improve it. For example, if there are high numbers of visitors exiting the site from the same page, you might want to look at that page and try to figure out why.

A good statistics package will tell you the most popular entry pages and exit pages of your site. Harvesting this information is just the start; knowing what to do with it is something else.

There are two web sites that contain valuable information on this topic. The first is at www.marketingexperiments.com. This site takes real products, money, and web sites of actual companies, and tests everything from e-mail marketing to page design, looking for better ways of using the Web more productively. And the best part is that the site is absolutely free as of this writing. The company being tested pays the costs of the testing. Companies and actual products are not named, but the test findings are real-life results.

The second site is at www.drillingdown.com. This site deals with the long term. The researchers study customer life cycles and how to keep them coming back again and again. They also look at return on investment (ROI) of your site. They will show you how to track cost per customer and cost per visitor to get the most bang from your buck from each and every visitor. Most of the site is free, but there are a few items for sale as well.

Should You Be on the Internet?   Now that we've explored the web site process, the next question to ask is: Do you belong on the Internet? Perhaps the prices and the struggle of creating a web site scare you. If you aren't totally committed to this medium yet, here's some discussion to get you up to speed.

Do you sell to the world, or do you do business locally? Even local business can benefit greatly from a Web presence. The smaller the town or area, the easier it is to direct customers to your site. Newspaper, radio, TV, brochures, and business cards should all include your web site address. Include an area in the site where customers can e-mail you with questions or comments. You can also put your brochure, catalog, price lists, maps, and anything else you can think of on your page. Realtors, travel agents, and craftspeople love web pages.

Can you create your own web site? I created my entire site in Adobe PageMill 3.0 (there is a 160-page user guide, and it is very easy to use). Software cost about $65. I created one simple page and took it to my Internet service provider to make sure it would work before I did the whole site in this program.

Had I used a $60 per hour or more Web design service, my site would have cost approximately $6,500 to $10,000! I realized a pretty good savings by doing it myself. Was the site pretty and professional looking at first? Not even close. However, over time your site will evolve and improve, as mine has. It's better to have something bad out there working than nothing at all. I sat down and forced myself to learn how to do a web site because it was the only way I was going to have one. The other very important advantage of doing my own site was that I found what worked and what didn't.

Do you have the time to maintain the site and keep it up to date? Nothing will turn people off more than a site that never changes. Why keep coming back if there is no new information? If you're going to have a web site, you must make it interactive with your potential customers. They must have a reason to return over and over again. They may visit your site many times before they finally decide to buy from you.

Here are a few strengths and weaknesses of the Internet.

Strengths of the Internet

Look, I'm BIG: You can look as big as Microsoft, Coca-Cola, or anybody else out there. No one can tell by looking at a web page how big the company is.

Cost: (You'll find this in the negatives, too.) If you can create and maintain your own web site (I did mine, so how hard can it be?), the cost is less than any other media. It is literally pennies each for the vast numbers of potential customers you'll reach. No other medium can reach the entire world 24 hours a day, 365 days a year.

Size of your message: My web site, located at www.smalltown marketing.com, has 400 pages at present. Each year it grows about 100 pages or so. Some sites have over 5,000 individual pages. Try keeping those all linked together.

Catalog: If you have numerous products, where else can you have a full-color catalog of your entire line, available to every person, anywhere in the world? What would the cost be to print six billion full-color catalogs?

What about updating that catalog? Studies of quick printers show that 25 percent of all printed materials are thrown away. The information becomes outdated, products are discontinued, or the company moves or changes phone numbers. Discarding that much information can be a tremendous waste to a company. By using the Internet, a few quick keystrokes and your catalogs are current again, and customers never know the difference.

Internet brochures: You can put your brochure online and customers can print it out on their own printers, saving your hundreds of dollars in printing costs. The other great value is that your online brochures will never be out of date. If you add or delete products, you can change the brochure almost immediately. You can also use video images to demonstrate your products, complete with narration and music. If you can imagine it, it can be done on the Internet.

Complements other advertising: Put your Web address on every piece of literature you have. Customers who find your web site brochure or catalog will be directed to your site. Add a teaser phrase to your ads, such as, "Visit our web site at www.yourcompany.com for unadvertised specials and discounts."

Business cards, stationery, brochures, and every ad you run in any medium should contain your Web address somewhere. Does your local chamber of commerce have a web site? See about a listing or banner there of your site address. Utilize all your resources to direct people to your web site. Use your site to call them to action and order your products online or visit your place of business.

Business help: If you don't have a web site, or have no desire to have one, I would still encourage you to get Internet access at home or at work. The amount of *free* helpful business information is enormous and growing every day. The Small Business Administration has business plans and marketing information. Individual industries have web sites to help you with almost any question.

Weaknesses of the Internet
Size: The very thing that makes the Internet so attractive to business is also one of its biggest weaknesses. Twenty thousand sites per month

join the Internet family. It is so big, it's easy to be lost in a sea of information.

Cost: If you aren't able to create and maintain your own site, the costs involved can be high. Web site design can range anywhere from $30 per hour to several hundred dollars per hour, depending on the quality and experience of the designer.

Look at your competitors' web sites. Usually the web designer has a little logo or link at the bottom of the page. Nothing is wrong with that person designing your pages, too. Perhaps he or she can improve on what was done for your competitor or make something entirely different.

Internet service provider (ISP): The Internet service provider (think of it as the switchboard at the phone company) will charge a monthly fee for hosting your site. Usually this cost is based on the size (amount of computer memory required) of the site. The more space it requires, the higher the cost.

It never ceases to amaze me how people look only at the cost of a service. I was talking to a businessman who was bragging about how little he was paying for his site. ISPs are businesses just like any other; they need to show a profit to survive. The expenses of an ISP are very, very high. Will your low-cost ISP be able to stay in business cutting its prices? Will it be able to maintain the equipment? The answer is usually no.

If the ISP goes out of business, what happens to you, and to your site? If you can't get your site out of the ISP's system, you may have to pay to create it all over again. In addition, if you change providers, you may have a problem with your search engine links. You'll need to put a "We've moved" page up to direct people to your new home. Make sure you look at more than price when selecting an ISP. It must have the best available equipment, be up all the time, and operate flawlessly.

Be very careful in selecting an ISP. Price is the very last consideration I would have. Ask to speak with some customers who are doing well with the service. Talk to them and see if they are satisfied with the customer support.

Register a Domain Name   A domain name is a name you own and only you can use. For example, www.nbc.com is exclusive to the National Broadcasting Company. It will help your advertising greatly if your domain name is either distinctive or descriptive (or both), and it should be easy to remember.

My site name is www.smalltownmarketing.com (if you just type smalltownmarketing.com, the site will come up, too). It's easy to remember, and it describes what you'll find at the site. If I didn't have my own registered domain name, my address would be www.avicom .net/smalltownmarketing/index.html. How easy is that to remember?

Leave out or mistype any part and you wouldn't find my site. This is a major problem with free page sites: The address must be in front of the customer. They couldn't possibly remember it.

Hits/Visitors   This is more a misunderstanding than a weakness. We read from time to time of a web site getting 1,000 hits a day or 10,000 hits a day or 100,000.

What is a hit? Most people think it's a person who came to your site. No, it isn't. That's called a unique visitor.

A hit is an exposure to an element on one page of your site. When a person visits your site and goes to a specific page on that site, that is one hit. If the page has three graphic elements on it (photos, for example), each graphic on the page counts as a hit. So now our visitor has seen one page and we have four hits (one for the page and one for each of the elements). The visitor moves to the next page, and bingo, four more hits, and so on. If we have enough pages and the person stays long enough, that one visitor may do 1,000 hits by him- or herself.

There is nothing deceitful about telling folks your page is getting a lot of hits. Just make sure you aren't inferring that hits are individual visitors. New web sites talk about hits, and established sites with lots of traffic talk about unique visitors.

Credit Cards: Are They Safe on the Internet?   I go into a restaurant, enjoy a nice meal, and give the waitress my credit card. She takes the card and processes it; at closing the transaction information goes to whoever makes the bank deposit, then to a teller at the bank, then to someone at the credit card clearinghouse, then to another teller at the issuing bank, then to a Dumpster in downtown Philadelphia, and finally to a landfill. How safe is that?

That restaurant argument is the very same one that went around when the first credit card was introduced in the mid-1960s. People were sure clerks in stores would steal the numbers and the cardholder would be liable for the purchases. People would never even consider giving a credit card number over the phone.

Do you really believe there is someone out there with the equipment needed and the expertise waiting to get your card number? To do what? Buy a Rolls-Royce? Most of us don't have a credit balance large enough to buy a tank of gas.

If you tell me a hacker wants to break into Citicorp and steal 10 million credit card numbers, that I'll believe before I'll believe they're lying in wait for me to make a transaction. If you are really concerned, get a credit card with a small limit and use it only on the Internet. Under current law you're liable for only $50 on a stolen credit card.

Identity theft is a serious problem. Each day we read about some laptop with credit card or Social Security numbers being lost, stolen, or misplaced. We live in an imperfect world, but business goes on and I would encourage you not to place a lot of weight on this problem. There are many online safeguards that protect both the customer and the merchant, and I would encourage you to use them as your business dictates.

If you are accepting credit cards online, it's even more critical that your site be up 24/7/365. If your site is down for any reason, you are out of business. What would you do if your business doors locked several times a day?

The Last Word on the Internet   Internet commerce is on the move, and you may want to consider being a part of it. Does promotion of your web site pay off? Consider this:

In 1994, for every dollar direct marketers spent on Internet advertising, $4 in sales were generated. By 1997, ad-to-sales ratios had almost doubled: For every dollar direct marketers spent in advertising online, on average, $7 in sales were generated, according to a report entitled "Economic Impact: U.S. Direct Marketing Today— A Landmark Comprehensive Study, 1997." I don't know about you, but I could live with those numbers. This study was commissioned by the Direct Marketing Association (DMA) and conducted by The WEFA Group. The complete study may be purchased by contacting the DMA's Book Distribution Center at 301-604-0187.

Considering this is a 10-year-old study, where are we today?

"E-commerce is becoming more mainstream," said Jeffrey Grau, senior analyst at the research firm eMarketer. "A larger segment of the population is buying online, and people are buying more things than they have in the past."

U.S. Internet Sales Pass $100 Billion   Investment firm Cowen & Co. put the total U.S. Internet sales figure for 2006 slightly higher at $108 billion, predicting that it will hit $225 billion by 2011.

In summary, the Internet is good, bad, and everything in between. Should you be on it?

Here are 10 questions to ask:

1. Do you print and distribute large amounts of materials to customers? Remember that 25 percent of everything printed ends up in the Dumpster.

2. Do you provide documentation or specifications of your products to customers? These items can change rapidly as products improve. With the Internet all documentation is always up to date.

3. Would customer service and support costs be reduced if information were available on demand? The more customers call, the more valuable it would be to have a frequently asked questions page and a way for customers to ask questions by e-mail.

4. Do you sell by direct mail or mail order? You might want to consider e-mail marketing to cut costs here.

5. Can your business be easily described by a keyword? The more distinctive you are, the better the Internet is at producing customers.

6. Do you ship products to customers? Online ordering can increase sales.

7. Do you sell directly to customers? There is no better way to give them every conceivable piece of information about your products and services.

8. Is there something that makes your product unique? If you have to tell a detailed story or educate customers about your product, few media do better than the Internet.

9. Can your product be easily shipped to a customer? Books, crafts, and information are all great products for the Internet.

10. Do you produce catalogs of your merchandise? Put your entire catalog online for a fraction of the printed cost.

If you answered yes to eight or more of these questions, you should consider an Internet presence.

Publicity

The last topic of the media mix is publicity—how to get it and how to use it. Here are four things you need to do immediately, if you haven't already:

1. Most newspapers have an assignment editor, who assigns the stories to the reporters. Write him or her a letter explaining your expertise in your industry and that if a story about your industry comes along, you would be happy to provide information to the reporter. Enclose your card with your name and address, phone,

e-mail, and so on. If you don't have a business card, you can buy blanks at most office supply stores and print them out on your home printer. If you are truly serious about your business, have cards professionally made.

2. Contact civic groups in your area that might be looking for speakers. Many have weekly or monthly programs. Most won't let you do an infomercial for your company, but they will allow you to talk about your industry. For example, I've spoken at many of the Kiwanis Clubs in the San Diego area. What was my topic? "How to Market Your Kiwanis Club," of course. Do you have a fear of public speaking? We all do. Take a Dale Carnegie course—that was my answer. Your local adult education office may also offer public speaking courses. Toastmasters is another great group to help you with public speaking. Find your nearest chapter at www.toastmasters.com.

3. Most newspapers and magazines have a masthead near the front of the publication that lists the publisher, editor, and specific editors of various sections of the publication. For each publication and radio/TV station in your advertising area, start a record of the following: web site; name and title of contact person; publication or station name; if radio, type of format (rock, talk, country); address, phone, and zip code; areas of interest for which they are responsible (city news/county news/features/sports); publication demographics as they pertain to your business; deadline dates, if any; any past articles that have to do with your industry or business in general; any past articles about your competitors; and a record of all letters and discussions with the publication/station.

4. Have some press photos done. Always use a professional photographer. Don't save money by doing it yourself. Take pictures of your staff and key employees, your business, products or service (in use if possible—action shots sell), and your building or storefront if you have one. For your portrait shots, use a

light background if possible, which will reproduce better in the newspaper. If news breaks and you need to seize the moment, you need to be ready with the information the media need or they will find it elsewhere.

Press Releases: What Are They and How Do You Use Them?
Press releases are announcements sent to newspapers, magazines, and radio and TV stations containing newsworthy information about your company, service, or industry. They are written in a very specific format, which I will cover in a moment. First, let's deal with the steps of preparing the information for a press release.

1. *It must be news.* No medium is going to run a free commercial for you. There is a thin line where news ends and a commercial begins. The newspaper or station wants to stay on the news side, and you want to be on the commercial side. If you can't explain why it's news, then it may not be and they won't print it.

2. *Who gets the release?* Remember the list I asked you to make earlier. That's the group who gets the final version.

3. *No more than three pages maximum.* An editor may receive several press releases in a day. If the article is too long, it probably won't even be read. Be brief and to the point. Blaise Pascal said, "I have made this [letter] longer than usual, only because I have not had the time to make it shorter." Take the time to be concise.

4. *Who, what, when, where, why, and how?* The news release should answer all of these. Who did what? Who does it affect? How does it affect them? Why does it affect them and not someone else? When will it affect them? Where will it happen?

5. *Quotes.* Experts in your industry add weight and credibility to the story, but don't overuse quotes.

6. *Can you write?* Many small business owners have to write their own releases. If you don't feel comfortable writing the release

yourself, find a professional to help. If none are available, look to the English department at the nearest college or university.

7. *Prepare a media kit.* If there are studies, illustrations, or pictures that support your story, include them. They may not be used, but they will strengthen your position. Have all the photos, brochures, company history, past news articles, awards, and anything else you can think of that will enhance your image in the eyes of the press.

8. *Prepare your staff.* There is nothing worse than a reporter showing up on the day you are gone and getting some off-the-wall quote from one of the staff who has no idea what's going on. Have someone at your business make an appointment when you can meet with the reporter, or designate a spokesperson to act on your behalf who is familiar with the press release and what you want to accomplish. Make sure all employees are familiar with the media kit.

9. *There are no guarantees.* If the newspaper decides to run a story on you, there are no guarantees that it will appear when you want and where you want. Your story may be buried back by the classifieds somewhere. Worse yet, they may have gotten the other side of the story from your competitor. They may gloss over your best stuff and just print some statistics and not even mention your name.

10. *Follow up.* For a newspaper, follow up in one or two days. Don't ask, "When are you going to print my story?" Instead, ask if there are any questions you can answer. Is there any additional information you might be able to provide?

What Should a Press Release Look Like? A press release has a very specific format. The cover page is usually on company stationery. If you don't have any, typeset the company name, address, zip code, and phone number in the upper left-hand corner of an $8\frac{1}{2} \times 11$ page.

Margins should not be less than three-quarters of an inch or more than one inch from all sides. In the upper right-hand corner type the following:

NEWS RELEASE

Contact for Editorial Information:

Your Name, Your Title

Phone Numbers

The first line flush left, all capitals should be:

FOR RELEASE ON [Insert date]

or

FOR IMMEDIATE RELEASE

Next, announce the news with a clear, simple headline, in upper- and lowercase type, centered on the page, such as:

New Book Details Marketing Plan for Business Owners in Small Towns

Start the news with the location and current date. The first paragraph would look like this:

Bozeman, Mont., July 6, 2008—Small Town Marketing.Com announced today a new book entitled *How to Market, Advertise, and Promote Your Business or Service in Your Own Backyard,* by Tom Egelhoff. The book is aimed at small businesses in locales where marketing and advertising agencies are either unavailable or not affordable. The book provides a step-by-step marketing plan designed for the special challenges of marketing a business or service in a small town. Also included are chapters on small town business promotion, small town advertising, small town success principles, and home-based business success principles. This book is available for immediate download at www.smalltownmarketing.com.

Tell the Story in the First Paragraph   When you write the first paragraph, keep in mind that it may be the only part the paper uses. The first paragraph should be able to stand alone without any of the rest of the release. Use additional paragraphs for additional points in order of importance and priority.

Each paragraph is flush left, no indents; put a double space between paragraphs. If the release is going to continue to the following page(s), place the word "More," in parentheses, centered at the bottom of the page.

At the end of the release, put three number symbols or pound signs centered on the page:

###

The news release alone is enough for an entire book. Visit the public library and you'll find several books on the subject. Check with the local newspaper. Sometimes papers will have prepared a news release outline that details the way they would like to receive a news release. Also ask how they would like to receive it. Some editors prefer e-mail or MS Word document. You will have a much better chance of getting it published if you follow the preferred format.

Here are a few additional points to keep in mind. Can you tie your business image to any national event—the World Series, the Olympics, or the Super Bowl, for example? What about something going on in your state? Do you have an unusual product or service? Do any of your employees have a personal story that relates to your business? Remember, emotion sells.

Damage Control   There comes a time in every business when something negative happens. My parents were in the florist business. I remember when our dog bit a customer. Fortunately for my parents, this was during a time in the country when people weren't looking for a reason to sue each other. We treated her on the spot and gave her some free merchandise and an apology and that was the end of it. In today's society, we would probably be looking at a significant lawsuit, the certain death of the dog, and possibly the end of the business.

You are never going to know what will happen or when. We couldn't have foreseen that dog bite, but we could foresee something like pesticides on the flowers injuring someone, or a delivery person hitting a pedestrian.

I don't want you to feel that you must consider every possible accident that could ever happen in the universe. But look at your business, as well as your industry. Are there specifics in your business that could be a potential for bad publicity?

Many companies create hypothetical situations and plan the necessary media response even though they have no reason to believe it will really occur. It's the Boy Scout motto: "Be prepared."

The Last Word on Publicity   The advantage of a small town is that you won't have several thousand businesses trying to outdo each other in the quest for news space. You'll have only a few hundred. Take a good look at your business and what's going on around you, and make some news.

Summary of Advertising in General

If there is one mistake small town businesses make more often than any other, it's "Whatever is left over in the budget we'll use for advertising." Marketing and advertising are an investment, not an expense. It surely seems like an expense to me when I'm writing the check, but trust me—it's not. Without enough money put aside for advertising, your sales can go down, and suddenly you have fewer resources with which to promote your business.

When do you advertise the most? For most businesses, it's the first day of business. Don't you have a grand opening, balloons, flyers, ads, on-site radio remotes, contests, and prizes? In Bozeman, Montana, the population turns over every 7 to 10 years. That means a lot of new people are coming to this part of the country, and others are leaving. Almost everyone who moves to your little backyard has to find a barber, dentist, grocery, shoe store, veterinarian, and clothing store, to name just a few.

Did the income from sales pay for this grand opening? No, it didn't. You have no sales yet. You advertise most when you need business, because that's the whole purpose of advertising: to build traffic to your business. You advertise even more when you don't need business, because good times don't always last. Because of population turnover, your name always needs to be out there.

An average cost of advertising is usually 1 to 5 percent of gross sales, which can vary according to location, local advertising rates, and your particular industry. Car dealers need more advertising than funeral homes.

Let's look at the four basic strategies of successful advertising:

1. In order to be successful, your advertising must provide a consumer benefit or solve a problem. Remember, you are selling benefits, not features.

2. That benefit or solution must be wanted by the consumer. In the case of the hula hoop, 50 million people didn't realize they needed it until marketing and advertising created that need.

3. The product or service you are offering must be tied directly to that benefit or solution. Customers buy products because the products make them feel a certain way. You sell emotion.

4. The benefit or solution must be distinctly communicated through media advertising. In other words, be clear, forget the advertising glitz, and make sure the message isn't lost in the ad. Comedy is good and often memorable. Just be sure you are truly funny before you try it.

A small-budget advertiser doesn't have the deep pockets to develop big advertising campaigns. Sometimes you need to break the rules to be noticed. Avis did it by admitting it was "Number 2" in the car rental business (behind Hertz), and therefore "We Try Harder." Now Avis has revived that winning promotion once again, and we will see where it will take the company.

Budget-conscious advertisers must achieve top results for their advertising dollar. Expand your dollars by adopting some creative techniques. Here are 25 tips I've used over the years to help small businesses get a jump on the competition. I hope these will help you:

1. Radio, newspaper, and magazine specialists will frequently give free help in developing an advertising strategy: things like demographic information and money-saving ways to produce your ads. If you need demographic information, go to www.census.gov for local info on your area. You can also find simple info about your area by entering your zip code at www.bestplaces.net. There is also a ton of demographic information at www.melissadata.com.

2. Place your ads in off-hours or in unusual locations for less. Many times you can still reach your target market with these spots. Instead of a one-time big-splash ad, be consistent with frequent small ads that work. We did this with the video store in San Diego. Several small ads of one inch appeared in each section of the newspaper every day. It didn't take long for the name to take off.

3. Monthly magazines sometimes have unsold ad space at the end of the month they will sell at a discount. Your local library may have a copy of *Ulrich's Periodicals Directory.* This is an annual listing of trade industry magazines, mainstream magazines, and newsletters where you can find the ones that will reach your target market for a smaller investment.

4. If you have an 800 number, put it in every ad for immediate response and feedback. My toll-free number forwards to my cell phone after three rings, so I never miss touching base with a client. Also put your web site and e-mail addresses in your ads, and don't forget to put your web site address on your answering machine.

5. Test advertising in the classifieds under such headings as "Items to sell." These ads may not draw as many customers as a more expensive display ad, but several calls can indicate a winning product or ad copy for future display ads.

6. Other than TV, most media will create your ad for free. If they don't, see if you can barter for the cost of ad production or even the ad itself. Maybe the TV station needs painting in exchange for producing an ad about your paint store.

7. An example of piggyback advertising would be the ads you receive with your monthly credit card statement. Incidentally, I always like to enclose my brochure and business card with my check back to them. I sincerely believe that the people opening those bill payments do not like that job, and might go to my site and get inspired to start their own business.

   Is there a business in your town that sends out a lot of bills? Banks are ideal for this, particularly if you are a nonprofit. Most people carefully review their monthly bank statements and might just fill out a pledge card. Ask if you can put a small flyer in with the bank's statements and split the cost of postage, or pay a small fee to be included in the mailing.

8. Split advertising costs with the people who sell to you. Many bars and restaurants have signs that feature the names of popular soft drinks the business carries. Vendors and manufacturers are always looking for exposure. Let them know you carry their products, and have the vendor pick up part of the ad cost.

9. Are there up-front advertising discounts for cash? Since advertising is usually a long-term investment, I would suggest negotiating terms for one year's worth of ads instead of a one-time break. In TV you might be able to get a deal on production costs for a longer commitment with the station.

10. Consider advertising in regional issues of national magazines. The costs are lower, and you can still reach your target market. *TV Guide* is a good choice. It stays around for at least a week. *Time*, *Newsweek*, and *U.S. News & World Report* may stay in local doctors' offices for years. If there is a particular magazine that you feel fits with your target market, get the advertising phone number from the masthead (it is usually in the first few pages and lists the publisher and others) and contact the advertising department.

11. Share ad costs with neighbor businesses. Video stores and pizza parlors are natural partners. Have coupons to each other's stores or share the cost of printing flyers.

12. Advertising salespeople are going to talk in terms of cost per thousand viewers or listeners. This is an okay way to estimate the size of the market you will reach. However, think in terms of cost per customer. If an ad costs $40 and it produces two customers who each spent $10, what happened? You lost $20 on your advertising. It did not pay for itself. Ask yourself this question: Will more produce more? If I spend more money, will I make more money?

    Consider the following. Try reducing the size of your ads or the length of your radio spots. A 60-second radio spot does not cost twice as much as a 30-second spot. But there is also no study I am aware of showing that you will get twice as many customers from a 60-second spot than from a 30-second spot.

If you truly need a full minute to tell your story, then by all means use it. But I would test 30-second ads to at least prove to myself that they are too short. Going with smaller ads or shorter spots will allow you to do more ads, which normally pull more customers. It's better to be there every day with small ads than every month with one big one.

13. Simple generic ads are easier to produce than very specific ads and can be used longer. Remember that the message is more important than the messenger. Don't try to produce ads that win awards; just produce ads that get results.

14. When you think of your ideal customer, does a particular person pop into your mind? This is the person you want to speak to in all your advertising. Aim your ads to talk directly to people like that individual.

15. What will suppliers give you in the way of point-of-purchase materials (posters, stand-ups, handouts, etc.)? Some have excellent display racks you can use. Many also have interesting items to give away. I have a radio show affiliated with Fox, and we gave away doctors' bags from the popular TV show *House*. They were a big hit and brought a lot of new listeners to the show.

16. Some national companies like Coke and Pepsi provide outdoor signs for businesses. There are also indoor lighted signs you write on with special markers to advertise your special offers.

17. Can you sponsor a community event—a fun run, golf tournament, or other event that will be well publicized in the community? Your name may not be prominently displayed, but sometimes the positive exposure in the community will bring in new customers. Make sure you attend the event and let people know you are one of the proud sponsors.

18. Small businesses can seldom afford saturation advertising. You must be selective in the media that reach your customers. Pin your ad reps down and make them show you exactly how their media reach your target audience.

19. Exploit the media you choose. Remember, as long as advertising is paying for itself it doesn't matter how much it costs. Radio would not have been the medium to sell the hula hoop no matter how good a buy the ad might have been. However, if your message is verbal, you don't need TV. Use the strengths of TV, radio, billboards, direct mail, and newspapers to show off your product or service to the fullest at the most economical price.

20. Consider direct mail. A letter and brochure before customer contact can open doors and increase business. An IBM study concluded that selling time can be reduced from 9.3 to 1.3 total hours with direct mail advertising. A Sales and Marketing Executives International study showed salespeople who used direct mail went from eight orders per 100 cold calls to 38 orders per 100 cold calls.

21. There are ads that look like actual stories in the newspaper. They have an attention-grabbing headline and well-written story. They will have "Advertisement" in small print at the top of the article. Develop a good headline, and 50 percent more people will read the article than would read an ad of the same size. Most will miss the word "Advertisement" at the top, but even if they see it, as long as the message is a good one a sale will happen.

22. You can't match larger competitors like Wal-Mart dollar for dollar, but you can use unusual approaches (like the Avis motto or the Coin Mart Jewelers idea), while also using color, music, slogans, and humor (just make sure you're really funny), or media selection to win your market away from the big guys.

23. Your mainstream advertising must always pay for itself. However, there are some other advertising opportunities that might

be more costly but can reach customers who don't read the newspaper or watch much TV. The list of where you can't advertise is probably shorter than where you can. Today, you find advertising in rest rooms and on parking meters, taxis, balloons, park benches, blimps, and grocery shopping carts. Don't forget community bulletin boards, movie theater ads, or weekly newspaper shoppers.

24. Key your ads. Put something in the ad that will let you know which medium it came from. Put a code on coupons that will record the paper and date of the ad. In radio or TV, have customers mention the ad to get the discount. Ask each and every new customer how he or she found you.

25. Plan for a rainy day. During the year, put a small amount aside each month for emergencies. You never know when you'll need to react quickly to whatever the competition is doing. You must be able to capitalize on breaking national events or news regarding your industry. If negative things happen in your industry, you may need to respond quickly to make sure the right message is presented.

26. Always give customers more than you promised, and more than they expected. This is tip number 26 of the 25 you expected. Maybe this last one is the one you needed.

I hope these tips will help your business grow.

Not all of these tips will be relevant to your particular situation, but I hope they illustrate the importance of planning and controlling your advertising budget.

One more time before we leave this chapter: Advertising and marketing are what? Very good! Advertising and marketing are an investment, not an expense. Invest wisely and reap the benefits.

Step 8: Design a Marketing Calendar

N ow that you have all your marketing steps completed, it's
time to create your calendar for the first six months of the
year. Start *now*—don't wait until next January to set up
your marketing calendar.

The marketing calendar is a tool you will use to easily track all
your marketing and advertising efforts. One of the biggest mistakes
that small business owners make is stretching themselves too thin.
They decide to have a sale on the spur of the moment without thinking about other expenses or conflicts. They do this because they have
no guide to show them what they have already done and what they
have planned for the future. The calendar will also provide you with
a thumbnail sketch of the spacing between events. It will keep you
from having too many sales or sales that are too close to each other.

You can also check your schedule against other events planned
for your town or neighborhood. If you're a bar owner, you may be able
to capitalize on a local event such as a homecoming football game,
whereas a church social might empty out the place.

I like to set up a six-month calendar because it's long enough to plan for most events or promotions. A simple sale might have several components that can last weeks or months. You may need to bring in additional inventory or have an ad campaign designed and printed. The marketing calendar will show you how to track all the activities associated with any sale or promotion. Here's how to create one of your own.

How to Set Up and Design a Marketing and Advertising Calendar

Use a piece of 8½ × 14 legal-sized graph paper with boxes that cover the page. Or, if you have a spreadsheet program like Microsoft Excel, this is an easy form to create. This size works best and is easy to file and work with, but you could also use an 11 × 17 sheet if you need more space or larger printing. One of the long sides of the paper will be the top.

Start by drawing a heavy line dividing the paper in half horizontally. Then measure two and a half inches from the left side of the paper and draw a vertical line from the top of the page to the bottom. In Excel, this will be your first column. Down this left side of the page is where you are going to write in the various events and actions.

Across the top of the page, starting at the vertical line you just drew, you are going to show the months, with the individual weeks underneath each month. It should look like this:

Marketing Calendar for June, July, and August

	June					July				August			
Event	2	9	16	23	30	7	14	21	28	4	11	18	25
Half-Off Sale					■								

		June				July				August		
Actions/Tasks	2	9	16	23	30	7	14	21	28	4	11	18	25
Half-Off Sale—Print Ads			███	███									
Half-Off Sale—Radio				███	███								
Inventory Shipment	███												
Half-Off Sale—Planning	███												

On the left side of the top half of the page, list the sales, promotions, and events you are planning for the next six months. On
the left side of the bottom half, list the various media you intend to
use: radio, TV, newspapers, magazines, flyers, direct mail, billboards,
or any other form of advertising in your arsenal. Also list tasks to be
done such as obtaining inventory.

Now you can begin setting up your calendar. If you own a retail
store, you would list things like half-off sale, anniversary sale, or
Mother's Day sale down the left side of the top half.

As you can see, a half-off sale is scheduled for the last weekend
in June. (You would either place an X or color in the box for the last
week of June.)

Next, go to the second half of the page, to the media you have
listed. You will want to run some newspaper ads to promote your
half-off sale. Since the half-off sale will be the last week of June, you
will want to start running newspaper and radio ads two weeks before
the sale to build traffic and interest in the upcoming sale.

Go down the left side of the page to print ads, move to the right
until you are under the middle two weeks in June, and place an X
or color in those boxes. In order to keep things organized, I would
suggest using different colors for each project. If you assign blue as
the color of your half-off sale, then use blue on all media and so forth
for the half-off sale in the lower half of the calendar.

The calendar also shows that you need to get inventory into the store for the upcoming sale and you have scheduled a planning meeting to discuss the advertising, budget, and any other strategies to make the sale successful.

With this type of calendar you will be able to go to any week of the six-month period, start at the top and go down and see what promotions are coming up and what media must be contacted and ads prepared. What merchandise to order, what signs to have made, and how much advertising to budget each month will all be on one sheet of paper that can be posted on the wall in your office. The calendar also keeps your employees updated on what's coming up so they can start promoting events to your customers.

The marketing calendar is an indispensable part of your total marketing plan. It will keep you on track and act as a constant reminder of where your business is and where you want it to go. It's also a great tool for planning your advertising budget. At a glance you can see all your promotions, advertising, and marketing on one sheet of paper.

Step 9: Execute Your Plan

Congratulations! You have finished assembling the various elements of your marketing plan. Now it's time to put it to work. You have your sales objectives and strategies, your target market, the types of promotions, the advertising message, and the media you will use. All that remains is to execute the plan as you have designed it.

One point that should be made is that as you execute your plan, some things may not go exactly as planned or happen as you hoped they would. Radio spots will be skipped, ads will be run with wrong dates or prices, or on the wrong days. Typos that camouflaged themselves through countless proofreading sessions will suddenly be glaringly visible.

All of these can and will happen, and as your plan is being executed you need to be ready to react when something goes wrong. Anytime you place responsibility in the hands of anyone who doesn't have a vested interest in your business, Murphy's Law (anything that can go wrong will go wrong) will take over.

If you are an experienced business owner, you know this all comes with the territory. However, if you are new to the business world, each setback and error can be exasperatingly frustrating. The best advice I can give you is to be ready for anything.

Step 10: Is Your Plan Working?

The final step is perhaps the hardest of all: an honest and objective evaluation of how the plan is, or is not, working. When you are close to your business, and these are your ideas, and they aren't working—even though every fiber of your being says they should be—it's tough on some people's egos to have to regroup and try another direction.

Please understand that no one knows how the public will react to anything. The pet rock pretty well proved that. People should be coming to your store but they aren't. Why not? What have you missed? Chances are you haven't missed anything. Chances are you just haven't waited long enough.

Marketing takes time to be effective. It is trial and error and testing, testing, testing. With the exception of sales, which are designed to increase traffic immediately, most good marketing promotions take anywhere from six to nine months before results are noticed. You are asking people to do something new—to consider your product or service instead of what they usually do. That process takes time.

Don't listen to anyone who has run a single newspaper ad one time and then tells you newspapers don't work—nobody came in. It's like playing baseball for the first time. You take one swing, miss, and then decide you can't hit the ball, so why play?

The best way to evaluate the plan is to do it in pieces, not as a total entity. Look at the various objectives you have set, such as sales objectives: How are your salespeople doing? Are sales edging upward? Or are they staying the same?

What about your marketing objectives and strategies? Are they on track? Is your positioning strategy working? Are you realizing any positive feedback on pricing, packaging, or your brand name? Are you getting any publicity from your news releases? Are the advertising media you chose producing any traffic? As you can see, there are many areas in a marketing plan that must be evaluated before the plan is scrapped in favor of something else.

Your plan will be in a constant state of evolution as you evaluate and improve the various components. Don't panic if results aren't immediate. The marketing plan has to grow. It starts as an infant and grows into a self-sustaining entity.

What's the Plan—If the Plan Isn't Working?

If there is overwhelming proof that the plan is not working, then what's the next step? At halftime, losing sports teams head to the locker room to make adjustments to improve their performance in the second half. Since the plan isn't working, we must have missed something. So here are some ways to find what's wrong and how to make adjustments.

The great thing about my marketing plan is that each part is dependent on the previous parts. You started with the business resume. This is the most likely place where mistakes were made. The hardest part of the plan is looking at you, and your business, coolly and objectively.

You may have embellished some part of the business or devalued another part. In either case, you are building a marketing plan on inaccurate information. If each subsequent part of the plan is building on wrong information, how can it possibly be successful?

The total success of this plan hinges on the accuracy of the first two steps: the business resume and the SWOT analysis. These two steps create a total snapshot of your business that you will use to present products to your target market. If you can't see your business plainly with your own eyes, how can you hope to present an image that customers will recognize?

I would suggest rereading the first two steps of the plan to see if you have missed anything. Ninety-nine percent of the time you have not described your business correctly and accurately. As soon as customers walk through your door, they instantly know that you are not as advertised and they walk back out.

Two other parts of the plan where mistakes are often made are not correctly identifying your target market and positioning strategy. If you are confident that you have correctly followed the first two steps, then you may have made a mistake in the evaluation of your target market. Recheck the sources of information used to identify them. If you based your plan on information from an owner in another city, you might want to talk to other owners to broaden the information. Perhaps the first source was in a nontypical market.

In the positioning chapter, I talked about the ways companies and products are perceived in the minds of the customer. Does your positioning statement make good sense? Is it believable to the customer? Have you found a strong position for your products and services? Have you successfully positioned your business away from your competitors?

Last but Not Least

If you are sure the target market and positioning are correct, then the next place to look is in the medium you have selected. Is your target market really there, and is your message beneficial to them? Remember, we said that people buy benefits, not features. Does your message carry an emotional hot button? If not, consider rewriting it from another perspective.

Review the plan again step-by-step. Does it seem to flow easily? Are there any parts that make you feel uncomfortable? Does the plan seem strong in some steps, but weaker in others? These little discomforts are emotional clues that you need to do more work on those problem areas of the plan. A little more research, a few more phone calls, and a little more reading and questioning can make all the difference.

Your plan is going to be constantly changing and evolving. This is the main reason that, hard as it seems to be, only you can do it. Only you can envision your plan at its eventual conclusion—a successful business.

CHAPTER
13

Small Town
Success Principles

The very strength of a small town is the key to your success in it. What is the strength of a small town? you ask. It's people. Small towns have people, whereas large cities have numbers, constituents, inhabitants—they are the public.

People in small towns not only know each other, but they also go out of their way to meet each other and introduce their friends to others. If you are a people person, you will have a tough time failing in most small towns. Small-town people were networking long before it became the buzzword of the new millennium.

Small-town people are forced to know each other by county fairs and church socials, funerals, their kids, civic and sporting events, and town meetings. They also understand that, in many cases, they are going to be together for a long time. Most of these folks would hate city life. Given a choice of living in New York City for the same price as in their small town, for most folks it's a no-brainer. They might like to visit New York—but live there? Not a chance.

If you are moving to a small town, here are four things to do to help your success:

1. Start meeting people as soon as possible. Local churches are the best place to start. These folks will welcome you with open arms. If they don't, I guess it's not really a church, is it?

2. You are in business, so where do the businesspeople meet? In the small farm town in Illinois where I grew up, a group of business-people meets every morning at a big round table in the back of one of the local restaurants.

   In Montana, where I live now, the local Rotary Club, Lions Club, and Kiwanis Club have a lot of the movers and shakers in town as members. The chamber of commerce has "Business After Hours" meetings once a month that are very popular with businesspeople. Join these groups and meet as many people as possible.

3. If you have difficulty meeting people, find the friendliest folks you can and build on them. Ask them to introduce you to their friends. And ask those friends and so on and so on.

4. Many successful businesspeople are happy to share their good fortune with the community by getting involved in the United Way, Junior Achievement, or other worthwhile causes. The better and more successful businesspeople in town usually support these groups. Join these groups and let them know that you are just like them—someone who wants to become actively involved in his or her new community.

If you are a longtime resident of your community, here are six things you can do to add to your success:

1. Become a kind of new welcome wagon for your town. That doesn't mean going around with gift baskets and welcoming each

new resident. When new businesses open their doors, or people are in your town scouting for a business location, meet as many of them as you can. They are going to be your new customers. Give them the best impression you can of yourself and their new neighborhood.

2. Support and encourage those around you. Whether you're the boss or the employee, you'll go farther as either with this attitude.

3. Try to be as optimistic as possible all the time. You'll find it's contagious to those around you. It's easy to sit around and gripe about everything in your life going wrong, but nobody wants to hear it. People gravitate toward positive people and away from the negative. When times are tough, they will probably turn to the most positive person they know for help or advice. Be that person. Be positive, and customers and employees will see you as a person they want to emulate and follow.

4. Show courage in both your business and personal life. They don't name highways for or build statues of followers. Be a leader in your community. Be the one to take the reins and get the project off the ground. Eighty percent of the results come from 20 percent of the participants. Be one of the 20 percent who make things happen.

5. Don't be afraid to seek the advice of others (provided they are qualified to give that advice). Don't ask some stranger on the next bar stool to evaluate your business—be selective in whom you ask for help. Try to get differing opinions whenever possible. Those opinions will force you to think about which option is best for your business. Consider all sides; when it feels right it usually is.

6. Always think, talk, and act like a professional. You will never be one unless you can see yourself as one. When we look at someone, we can't see the person's pedigree. We don't know what we're getting until we see some positive sign that shows this person

is someone we can learn from. What do you call a person who receives the lowest passing grade in medical school? You call him "Doctor." But, there are good doctors and bad doctors. It takes more than a diploma to be a professional.

As you walk or drive around your town or neighborhood tomorrow, take a really good look and appreciate what you have. Then set your sights on making it better. The rewards will be 100-fold.

Small Town Advertising

The basics of advertising are covered pretty extensively in Chapter 9, the media mix chapter of the marketing plan. What I want to do here is touch on a few points that are specific to small towns, and some final points to keep in mind as you put the word out to the world.

- Big city messages don't often work in small towns, so be careful of using premade ads from parent companies. An ad that shows a family on the front steps of a New York City brownstone may work great there, but no one in Judith Gap, Montana, is going to relate to it. Use the idea of these ads, but have them redone with a rural family on the back steps, and you'll have a winner.

- Small towns are people. Speak directly to one of those people in your ads, not the whole town. Each person will feel you are speaking only to him or her.

- Small-town folks are often portrayed as backward hicks or uneducated. They aren't. They are people just like you. Having an accent or talking slower than John Moschitta doesn't make you stupid. You must be truthful and absolutely believable in your ads if you want their business.

- Shouting and yelling may be effective in larger cities, but they seldom work in small towns. The only screaming or yelling that goes on in most small towns is at the Friday night football games.

- Talk is cheap. If your product is good, you're going to have to prove it here. If Missouri is the "Show Me" state, then welcome to "show me" towns.

- Many small towns are generational. That means there may be two or even three generations of families living there. If you can attract one generation, the others will most likely become your customers, too.

- In spite of the National Do Not Call Registry and state no-call lists, small towns are bombarded by telemarketers, just like large cities. Consider a coupon or a return card with your ad instead of an 800 number. Studies have shown that many rural people feel they are going to get a high-pressure sales pitch when calling an 800 number.

- Unlike large cities, small towns have more general demographics. A city may have an area of Eskimos you want to reach; you may want to create an ad just for them. In a small town your message must be more consistent in the different media you use, or it can be lost in the clutter.

- Testimonials are very powerful in small towns. If you can get an influential local person to endorse your product or service, your competitor is out in the cold. He or she will have to find another influential person to combat yours. In a small town that's not always easy to do. Line up several people if you can, and shoot the commercials as quickly as possible. That way you'll have them ready, and they can be released one by one over a long period of time.

- Keep every promise you make. Keep them even if you didn't make them. Advertising in a small town is dealing with real, honest, sincere people. They haven't been corrupted by the cutthroat tactics often used in big cities. They look for the best in people and expect the same in return. If you plan to do business in a small town, give your customers the level of service you'd want to receive. You'll be glad you did.

Small Town Promotion

How to Bring Them In

When you think of a promotion, most people think they're going to get something free. That isn't always the case, but people view a promotion as something good. Who does promotions? Car dealers are probably the world champions, followed closely by Circuit City type stores, and finally furniture stores. Why promote? It gets people in your store in a buying frame of mind. So what makes small town promotion any different from anywhere else?

The main difference is population numbers versus the cost of the promotion. A large city promotion may draw thousands, whereas a small town promotion might draw less than a hundred.

What those 100 customers actually purchase might not even cover the cost of the promotion, much less leave a profit. Any promotion is tricky, but small town promotion is even more dangerous.

Why do a promotion? What is the objective that you want a promotion to accomplish? One reason might be to stimulate business during a slow time of the year. Perhaps a Christmas sale in June might draw some attention. A promotion can be used to introduce a new product or service to the community, or show off a new facility after a move or remodeling.

When considering a promotion, the first item of business is almost always cost. How much is it going to cost us to "buy" these customers? And, make no mistake about it, you *are* buying them. You are giving them either a value or the chance at a value, such as a raffle.

The least expensive promotion is the cross-promotion. Get together with a noncompeting business and share the cost of the promotional advertising. This way you bring customers into both locations at half the cost.

Depending on your products, a drawing is probably the next best. Perhaps the manufacturer of the grand prize would be willing to provide some co-op advertising help. Be careful here, though; you may not see the co-op money for some time.

The most important thing about any promotion is proper exposure of your business or service to the right customer. There is nothing worse than spending a bundle on advertising and then seeing your store so full of customers that no one can even move, much less see anything.

You can't always control the number of people you're going to draw, but be prepared to move them through your business in an orderly and efficient manner.

Also remember that it's okay to sell things during a promotion. Sometimes business owners get so caught up in the celebration of the moment they forget that it's a business. It's okay to make a little money. Give customers the store tour another time. Put them in front of the merchandise and close the sale.

Holding a drawing is also a great way to generate a mailing list. I know what you're thinking: "That's pretty underhanded, don't you think?" Keep in mind that these people are at the promotion because they have an interest on what's going on there. They may not be buyers today, but keeping them informed with mailings may turn them into buyers in the future. Everyone likes to save money. Many of them will appreciate knowing about upcoming sales and promotions in the future. Caution: Depending on the type of promotion, you might just be developing a list of all the freeloaders in town.

The main point of promotion I want to make clear is to make sure you know what your objective is. Clearly define exactly what you want your promotion to accomplish. Set a measurable goal. Is it the number of customers you attract? Is it the amount of sales generated? Do you want to increase sales from current customers? Do you want to create increased sales after the promotion? Or are all of these your goals?

Set goals for your promotion, and measure what happens. If the promotion is successful, you may want to run it again later in the year. Promotions help maintain customer interest in your business. Good luck with yours.

Home-Based Marketing Success Principles

The Scenery Never Changes

Each day more people decide to join the 150 million who currently operate their own home-based businesses. These resourceful entrepreneurs do more business than the pharmaceutical industry, food industry, and consumer goods industry combined. The attraction of the Internet, low start-up costs, and flexible hours is taking many women out of the traditional workplace and turning them back into stay-at-home moms. When you take into account the cost of day care, transportation, lunches, and other expenses related to a traditional job, earning a little extra income by working from home offers a lot of advantages.

Home-based businesses are vastly different from storefront type businesses in that you're always at home—the scenery never changes. You get out of bed and walk a few steps, and you're at work. Does it seem too good to be true? As you might imagine, there are good and bad points to this arrangement.

Discipline Yourself at Home

Self-discipline is the heart of small business success, whether in a storefront or in a business in your home. If you can't make yourself do the work and ignore the little outside things that interfere with your goals, you will not be a success in any field. The key ingredient to that self-discipline is your dream or goal.

Successful people are successful because they have a dream or goal, and they will not be denied in their quest to make that dream or goal a reality. They work unbelievable hours, overcome hardships and setbacks, and persist no matter what. Read the biography of almost any famous businessperson, and you will read a story of failure after failure until success finally arrives.

Every successful person, from Bill Gates to Mother Teresa, got to where they are because they had the vision to see the goal and work toward it one step at a time, one day at a time.

This chapter deals with the areas you need to recognize and deal with to make your business a success. There are three initial areas:

1. Forced discipline.
2. Associations.
3. Vision of the future.

I'll discuss them one at a time.

Forced Discipline

To understand forced discipline, you must first understand the major differences between fear and desire. Fear is an extremely powerful inhibitor that will keep you from achieving your goals. Desire is a motivator that will propel you toward your goals.

Fear of Failure   In his book *The Psychology of Winning* (Berkley, 1984), Dr. Denis Waitley, PhD, uses the following example. Suppose I place a board two feet wide and 15 feet long on the floor. I put a $100 bill on one end and ask you to walk the length of the board and pick up the $100 bill. Would you do it? Of course you would. There is nothing to fear. Odds of failure are almost nonexistent.

Now suppose I put one end of the board on top of a 20-story building and the other end on an adjacent 20-story building. I put a rock on the $100 bill just to make sure it doesn't blow away. Now would you walk across the board? What have we added here? There is a very high penalty for failure, isn't there? Twenty stories straight down. The $100 is suddenly not a sufficient reward for the risk entailed.

Studies show more people fear public speaking than fear death. We fear what our friends or even total strangers will think of us so strongly that it affects our morals, standards, and principles. The fear of business failure, and our friends laughing at us if we fail, stops many people from even considering starting a business.

This isn't high school any longer, folks. If these people aren't helping you put food on the table for your family and don't support and encourage you, then they aren't your friends. It's that simple. Lose 'em! If you're successful, they'll be gone anyway. They aren't going to hang around with a successful person and have to explain to their friends why *they* aren't successful. It just isn't going to happen.

People who make $100,000 a year don't hang around with people making $18,000. So get on with the only life you'll ever have, and start making something happen for yourself and your family.

Desire—Just Do It   Desire is just as powerful as fear, but in a different way. Desire fights fear. When I was about six years old, I was at a swimming pool with my parents. I was playing in the shallow end of the pool when I suddenly slipped on the bottom of the pool and went under. From that day on I had a terrible fear of water. I never went into the water for any reason. You can imagine growing up in a farm community where everyone had a pond, stream, or some body of water nearby. It was years later in high school when I finally learned to swim and my fear of water miraculously disappeared. I thought to myself how stupid I had been and realized all the fun I had missed by not taking the necessary steps to overcome my fear.

My desire to learn to swim and be with my friends (girls primarily) finally pushed me to the point I had to overcome that fear. Desire was the answer. Once my desire became more powerful than my fear, the fear disappeared and my goal was accomplished. That is also how business success is achieved.

Let's get back to forced discipline, and you'll see how this all comes together. Forced discipline is fear. Self-discipline is desire.

Here's how they work:

As a kid growing up I lived under the shadow of forced discipline. My parents made all decisions for me, and if I didn't abide by those decisions, there were consequences. "Clean up your room or you can't go out and play." "Mow the yard or no car this weekend." "Be home by 11 o'clock or you're grounded." At school, "Do your homework or you won't pass." At work, "Be on time or you're fired." "Your evaluation was low, so no raise for you until you get the score back up." "I've got my eye on you."

Most people will stay where they are, in a job they despise, rather than face the fear of finding something better or more rewarding that may not work out. It's better to stay with a sure thing than have no job at all.

The government says, "Pay your income, property, sales, estate, excise, federal, state, city, county, and gas taxes or it's jail for you."

Is it any wonder we let fear overpower us? It's a lifelong habit we've acquired. Fear is quite literally a way of life for most people.

Go through your normal day tomorrow and see how often you must confront and overcome some form of fear. Forced discipline is easy. You have no choice in most cases. Fear is always an easy excuse.

That's why the majority of people in the American workforce spend all their time making someone else's dream come true instead of their own. Self-discipline, however, works to overcome the lifetime habit (and fear) of forced discipline. It's the only way to overcome it.

If you want to own your own business, you must have self-discipline. There is no other way. You must have a goal and work toward that goal every day. The goal or desire must be the total focus of your life in order for you to be successful.

In some cases, this may take a toll on your family. The extra hours of starting and running a part-time business are going to infringe on their time. Writing this book took time away from my family. I didn't wait until everyone else in the house was asleep to begin writing.

When I decided to write this book, I sat down with my wife and outlined the sacrifices we would both have to make in order to make the book a reality. I had to set a writing schedule, and with few exceptions I stuck to it. Here is a short example of how I used self-discipline to write this book:

Self-Discipline Plan

Goal One: What was the result I wanted? I wanted to sell 25,000 copies of this book. In order to even write the book, I had to have a goal of what was going to happen when it was done. I wrote down exactly what I wanted and expected from this book. I saw in my mind every day 25,000 books sold.

Goal Two: What was I willing to give in return for the 25,000 books sold? I was willing to, and did, spend at least 15 hours a week writing and researching for as long as it would take. In the case of this book it took about three years.

Goal Three: I had to establish an exact date for goal one: in this case, New Year's Day, 2010. By setting this date in my mind, my subconscious mind would work every day to make that date happen. I would be pushed to market, advertise, and do whatever was necessary to have 25,000 books sold by New Year's Day, 2010.

Goal Four: I created a definite plan of how I was going to sell those books. I wrote a complete marketing, promotion, and advertising plan to make my dream happen. Each day I had a schedule for the number of calls to make, letters to write, and e-mails to send.

Goal Five: I wrote out a clear, concise statement of the first four goals in as much detail as possible. I tried to list every conceivable problem I might encounter in reaching my goal and how I would overcome each problem. Each day I had specific tasks to accomplish. I needed to see some form of success each day as I moved toward the completion of the book. Even if I wrote only 10 words that particular day, I wanted to make sure they were the best 10 words ever written in the entire history of writing.

Goal Six: I read the statement created in goal five every morning and every evening. I taped short portions of the goals on the bathroom mirror, the dinner table, and the rearview mirror of my car (leaving enough room to see, of course). As I read these goals, I saw in my mind that they were beginning to happen. Suddenly I had a chapter finished, then another and another. This is how self-discipline really works. Your subconscious mind can't tell the difference between what is real and what is vividly imagined.

Don't we create imaginary fears in our minds? If we do, then why can't the opposite be true? If we imagine positive successful things, our minds will go in that direction, and we will work toward fulfillment of those mental commands.

Desire for success is the only way to overcome fear of failure.

Associations

"It was the best of times; it was the worst of times." Excuse me as I paraphrase Charles Dickens' *Tale of Two Cities*. For purposes of this book, let's change the quote slightly to "They were the best of people; they were the worst of people." In a small town, or in the relatively small world of the home-based business, we know a lot of people. Strange as it may seem, a lot more people know us.

There's good news and bad news. The good news is that people with expertise, who know your field and/or can help you, probably will. The bad news is that people with absolutely no expertise about your business, who couldn't possibly help you, probably will try.

Friends or Foes   Remember the old saying, "Birds of a feather flock together." We tend to associate with people who think the same way we do. Smokers gravitate toward each other; bowlers, golfers, hunters, readers, bird-watchers, and gang members all flock together. So, are friends bad? No, friends aren't bad, unless they try to give you information they are unqualified to give.

If you want to learn to play golf, do you join the local bowling league and start asking bowlers about golf? There may be some golfing bowlers, but doesn't it make more sense to go to the golf course, ask to see the golf pro, and take some lessons? Does it matter that the golf pro may be a complete stranger to you? The golf pro has the needed knowledge to assist you in accomplishing your goal—how to play golf.

Would you ask friends who have never played golf before in their lives to teach you? Why not?

After all, they're your friends, aren't they? They have your best interests at heart, don't they? They want to see you succeed, don't they? Do you see where we're going here? The road to the "hot place" is paved with good intentions. When my father decided to start his floral and landscaping business, he drove to the next town, met florists and landscapers, made friends, and hung around as long as they would let him. He watched how they designed things, what they charged, who their suppliers were, and how they ordered products. He learned from people doing what he wanted to do.

Some people he didn't ask: his father, his brother, his sister, his best friend. The reason he didn't ask any of them? They weren't qualified to advise him. They, as he, had no experience in the floral and landscaping business. Asking them would have been a waste of time.

"But I always ask my father," you protest.

I know, I know, you always get your dad's advice on every major decision. When I bought my first car I asked my dad for advice. He had bought a lot of cars. He had more experience than I did in that area. It was the same story when I bought my first house. But for legal advice, guess what—he recommended an attorney to me. He didn't try to give me legal advice. He knew he wasn't qualified to do that. Even your best friends will tell you, "Get a lawyer and sue the SOB." They don't say, "Let's go to court. I'll represent you."

Doesn't it seem strange that with something as serious as your business, the way you provide for your family, that your friends are more than willing to explain to you why your business ideas will or won't work? Worst of all, they do it under the guise of saving you from yourself. "We care about you." "We don't want to see you go down in flames." Of course, they don't know anything about your business, how it works, or your vision for it.

They can't see your business idea as you do, so it can't possibly work. Look at any of the great leaders of business or industry, and you'll see that somewhere in their lives, they were ridiculed and laughed at by people who didn't understand their vision.

Whether you love him or hate him, Bill Gates is a perfect example of a man with vision who rejected family advice, and endured all the computer nerd jokes, to rise to the pinnacle of his industry. I can imagine the IBM boardroom after signing the licensing contract with Gates for the DOS operating system. "Well, I hated to take advantage of that young man," they probably said. In fact, when Gates arrived for his first interview with IBM, he was so young looking he was mistaken for a mail boy and sent to the mail room in the lower area of the building.

Friendships are a very important part of our lives. I have the greatest respect for all my friends and I value their opinions on a variety of topics. Not asking them for advice about my business is not due to a lack of respect in any way. If your friends offer business advice, take it in the spirit in which it is intended. However, make sure you also get advice and opinions from people who have done what you want to do. Ask someone who has been there. They will give you the good and the bad. Then you can make a qualified decision and move your business forward.

Vision of the Future

The third area of home-based business success principles is being able to see into the future.

None of us truly knows what's around the next corner. Otherwise, why would the Psychic Friends Network need to ask for your credit card number? Shouldn't they know that already? If you're a parent, think back to when your children were about six months old. You're watching them crawl around on the living room floor. Do you picture them at age 30 still crawling around in diapers? Probably not. You picture them educated, with promising careers, happily married with the world at their feet. Every decision you make as they grow is based on where you want them to be as adults. Start picturing your business as your child. What do you see as its future?

Your Future Is Now   I know it's difficult when you look over at the corner of the room, and there's a card table and a telephone and that's your business. It's pretty hard to picture yourself as a threat to IBM, isn't it? You need to abandon that kind of thinking, and do it now—your future is *today*. Your child doesn't become an adult overnight, and the same will be true with your business.

The second area of concentration is to reprogram your mind to see your business as you want it to be every time you make a decision regarding your business. "How will this decision affect my business 5 years, 10 years, 20 years from now?"

What is the destination?

An airline pilot flying from New York to London can't see the destination for almost 99 percent of the flight. The secret of a successful business is knowing what you want the business to be, formulating a plan to make it happen, knowing where the destination is, and moving toward it. To paraphrase Earl Nightingale, success can be defined as the progressive, day by day, realization of a worthwhile goal or dream.

Move, day by day, toward the dream or goal of your business, seeing your business as you want it to be, and act like it's already there. Let me repeat that. *Act like it's already there*. Every decision, every sale, every contact says to clients and customers that this is a fast growing business. See your business as you want it to be; see the future.

Around the House

If you've never before had a home-based business, here are a few points to keep in mind.

Your Home and Yard

If customers have to come to your home for your products or services, make sure it's the kind of place they want to come back to. For example, if you smoke, stop (or start smoking outside). Nothing will turn some customers off faster than a stale smoke smell.

Your front yard gives the first impression when customers visit your business. Keep it mowed, trimmed, and as well manicured as possible. Remember, you are projecting a level of success to your customers. You should have the best-looking yard on the block.

Get a nice-looking front door, a relatively small expense. If you can't paint the whole house, paint the front and tell customers you are in the process of painting the rest. Avoid weird colors. Make sure that the first room the customer enters is neat and clean. If customers must walk through the house, make sure all pathways are clear of household items like laundry or toys.

Your Attire

"Hey! One of the reasons I wanted to work at home is so I wouldn't have to dress up anymore!" Your attire says who you are and what you think about your business and yourself. It says, I'm a success; even if I work at home, I'm still a professional. This doesn't necessarily mean a coat and tie or a dress and heels. It means neat, clean, and professional. Put yourself in the customer's shoes. The customer is wondering, Is the business in this house a business I want to deal with? Do I want to give this person my money? Am I confident that this business can do the job? And most important of all, will I do business with this person again?

Remember, working out of your house has the stigma of not being as good as a storefront business, although this attitude is becoming less prevalent as more and more people work at home.

Kids

Remember the old saying, "Children should be seen and not heard." This is a home-based business statement etched in stone. Children should not come into contact with your customers . . . period. Children do not commonly go to work with their parents in conventional storefronts, and the same should apply at home.

If you must meet with clients for extensive periods, arrange for someone to come in to handle the children or arrange for their care somewhere outside the home. Don't assume that your customers probably have kids and they'll understand.

Look at Me   I'll never forget going to a house in a nearby town to look at some crafts a woman was selling. She did beautiful work, but as soon as we walked through the door, her three children began yelling, running, and asking us who we were and what were we going to buy. "Look at me," one said as he tried to climb up the wall. It was a nightmare. We did place an order and I dreaded having to come back to pick it up. I wanted to have the check already written and to leave as quickly as possible.

Please understand, I am not antikid. I think kids are great. They're God's greatest gift. I'm used to them and how they act. Yelling and running are the normal things kids do. But to some people these activities are like fingernails on a blackboard. Unless it's absolutely impossible to do so, keep kids out of business situations and under control.

Phone

While we're on the subject of kids, if they answer the phone, teach them to do it in a professional manner. "Who is this?" "My name is Johnny, and I'm three" is not very professional. If you have one line into the house, make sure everyone who answers the phone knows a potential customer may be on the other end at any time. If you have two lines, make sure only you or designated persons answer your business line.

Fax Machine

With the advent of the Internet and e-mail, faxes are fast becoming the dinosaur of communication. But for certain types of businesses it's still important to have a fax machine. Contact customers and ask if they would like to be notified of certain changes in the company's products or services. Would they prefer notification by fax or e-mail? Make sure you give them a way to stop any unwanted faxes or e-mails from your business.

Faxes are a very inexpensive way to contact current customers about price changes, new products, and other information. One call can reach several customers using broadcast fax technology.

Use the fax as a substitute for the phone. Long distance and fax rates are lower after 5:00 PM and before 8:00 AM. Send faxes during these off-hours and save money. If you live on the East Coast, you can reply to a client or customer on the West Coast who simply needs specific information, or a yes or no answer, after 5 PM (at lower rates) when it's still midafternoon out West. You can place orders to suppliers this way, too.

Image

In the past few years a new industry has emerged—the image makers. These are people who are paid to make sure people and companies put their best foot forward in the business community. You probably don't need one of these folks yet, but you do need an image.

Image is easy on the Internet. Any kid in his bedroom can look and sound as big and good as IBM or any other big company. A few dollars' worth of software and a few keystrokes, and anybody can be a force on the Internet.

If you aren't on the Internet, that's okay. Look into the best stationery and business cards you can afford. If that's black ink on white paper, do it. You don't need fancy logos or unusual type styles. Keep it simple. Make sure that if you need to send a letter to a supplier for credit, or to a customer regarding payment, you look professional.

Brochures and Postcards

If you have brochures, make sure they tell your story briefly, but with enough detail to make the customer hungry for more information. If price is a consideration, qualify people asking for information. Contact them by phone and make sure they are legitimate customers and not just someone collecting information who may never buy anything.

Send postcards to potential customers with "Address Correction Requested" printed under your return address. Postcards cost about the same as bulk mail. There is no minimum that must be mailed. They are delivered first class instead of in three to four weeks with bulk mail. You will receive corrections to your mailing list free of charge, whereas bulk mail costs 26 cents for every card returned with a corrected address. Once your mailing list is clean, send brochures with confidence that they will reach the person they are supposed to reach.

Final Thoughts

Making a home-based business a success is one of the hardest jobs anyone can undertake. Many people will dismiss your job as a hobby and not really legitimate. Others will make fun of you and make it a point to ask, in front of others, "Have you made your first million yet?"

Unlike them, you have made the first steps in starting something they can only dream about. That dream will never come true for them, because they fear the one thing that will bring them success: taking the first step, and then the second and the third.

You are taking those steps now. Don't look back—they will all be out of sight soon.

SMALL BUSINESS MARKETING AND ADVERTISING IDEAS, TIPS, AND TRICKS

O ne of the great things about being older is having had the opportunity to work with some very intelligent and creative people over the past 40 years. It is in the spirit of a thank-you to them that I share this information with you.

Since the information wasn't mine to begin with, it only seems right to pass it along to you, as they did with me.

I hope the following tips will be helpful to you and your business.

1. Know Who Your Customers Are

- Describe the person most likely to want or need your product.
- Why should this person want to buy your product?
- When you know the motivation, you can target the product to the correct customer base.
- You can't sell a product until it is defined and positioned.

Note: A pharmaceutical company shelved a cold medicine because it couldn't correct the drowsiness it produced. Someone renamed it NyQuil and it was then sold as a bedtime cold medicine. It became the largest-selling cold medicine on the market. Just because your product is good doesn't mean it will sell. It must be positioned correctly. That's what marketing does.

2. Promote with Postcards

- First class postcard postage is 26 cents, about the same as bulk mail. Postcards convey a sense of urgency to the customer, who may not open and read your letter but will turn your postcard over and read it. (You have three seconds to get your message across. That's the average time people look at an ad.)

- Postcards will keep your mailing list clean ("Return Service Requested" or "Address Correction Requested"). First class postcards are returned and corrected free of charge by the post office. (Bulk mail corrections cost 26 cents each.)

With a postcard, your message is out in the open. Other potential customers will see it, too, not just the person to whom it's addressed.

3. Create a Survey

- Mail a survey to customers to find out what motivates them to buy.
- Where do they work? What magazines do they read? What is their age group?
- This information will tell you where and how to reach your targets.
- Offer a gift or discount for completing the survey.

4. Use a Two-Step Approach

Offer complimentary business-related information to potential customers.

- Step 1: Offer a free fact sheet to customers that shows your expertise.

- Step 2: Add these customers to your mailing list and mail to them often.

5. Say "Happy Birthday"

- Mail greeting cards to your customers (obtain dates from your survey in tip 3).

- Include a coupon or special offer for your product that they should give themselves as a gift.

6. Team Up with Another Business

- Share advertising costs with another company.

- Sharing costs makes high-quality printing and larger ads affordable.

- Can your product be teamed with another product? (An example might be motor oil packaged with your new funnel invention.)

7. Be Consistent and Committed

- Research shows advertising messages that are repeated will be remembered.

- Send multiple mailers to the same people.

- If you advertise, do it where you can afford to do it often.

8. Use the Telephone

- Test a new idea by phone before you commit to costly promotions.

- Response from 100 phone calls will be similar to 1,000 pieces of mail.

- You'll receive faster results at less cost, and you'll generate greater input and feedback.

9. Raise Your Prices

- Has your competition raised their prices? Maybe you should, too.
- Higher prices separate you from the crowd and imply that your product is better and deserves a premium price. BMW does not compete with Kia.
- Be careful in this area. The customer must see the value of the higher price.

10. Promote Trends or Current Events

- Can you tie your product or service to the environment, Olympics, or World Series?
- Gain valuable credibility and interest by your association with local civic and business groups.

11. Add Personalities to Your Business

- Use photos of yourself and/or your staff in your promotional materials.
- A quote or testimonial from the person pictured conveys friendliness and builds confidence in your company.
- Responses to seminars and programs are dramatically higher when photos are used.

12. Use Deadlines

- Make sure you print a time limit on all promotional materials.
- Watch your expiration dates. (Pay attention to which day of the month your offer ends. Are you losing an extra weekend of business?)

- If the last day of the month is a Wednesday, why not extend the sale through the following weekend?

13. *Capitalize on Fear of Not Having Your Product*

- For products that increase personal security, personal safety, or health, fear can be an effective business-boosting tool.
- If customers don't buy your product now, they will miss something—a discount, a premium, or a free gift. Fear of loss is always more powerful than expectation of gain.

14. *Use the Media*

- Send letters to local publications covering topics related to your business.
- Connect your product or business to some current event that is making news.
- Your name and business name will probably be used if your letter is printed.
- You will be perceived as an expert in your field.

15. *Make Advertising Last*

- Buy ads that last months, not minutes (yellow pages, for example).
- Put magnetic signs on your car or van. Don't forget the back of your vehicle—put signs on truck tailgates and rear windows, since most customers don't drive alongside and copy down the phone number or address. They are more apt to do so at a stop sign.
- If your vehicles have your company name and logo on them and are not being used on weekends, park them near high-traffic areas for billboard type exposure.
- Use clever bumper stickers or T-shirts.
- If you're printing an expensive color piece, ask the printer to quote the price of the house paper.

- Design the outside of the brochure to be permanent and the inside for future changes. That way you can print up large quantities (5,000 or more) of the outside only and have the printer keep them on hand. Then as your message changes you only have to print the inside.

- Although you will save by doing a large run in the beginning, you will also save by printing only what you need as your company changes. Avoid outdated brochures.

16. *Examine Promotional Materials*

- Make sure business cards, letterhead, brochures, and packaging materials are first class. This is not the area to spare expenses.

- What types of materials is your competition using?

- If you can't afford four-color brochures, use two or three colors. Use of color increases response by 26 percent.

- If you can't afford two colors, use screens.

Note: Using screens is a way to obtain lighter shades or tints. For example, suppose you are a florist and want red flowers around the borders of your brochure and black ink for the text. That's two colors. Pink is a 50 percent tint of red, not another color. You can have some pink flowers and some red flowers with little or no additional cost, depending on how your printer handles screens. This process will give the appearance of three colors: red, pink, and black. Use gray (a tint of black), and presto, a four-color brochure (red, pink, gray, and black) for a two-color price. It looks expensive but isn't.

17. *Make a Memorable Business Card*

- Make your business card a mini-brochure. If you need a map or other information, use the back of the card. Your card is there long after you're gone.

- One thousand two-color business cards retail for about $100, and it's worth it. (Use shades as described in the preceding tip, and have three- or four-color business cards.)
- How do your competitors' cards look? What message are they trying to convey?
- Give several cards to business associates who might be able to promote your business. Give a card to everyone you meet, and put one in every letter (even bills).

Note: Joe Girard, the famous car salesman, used to throw handfuls of business cards, like confetti, out of the upper deck at football games onto the expensive seats below. On the back of each card was a discount on any car bought the following Monday.

18. Say "Thank You"—Magic Words

- Thank customers with a special offer.
- Thank anyone who refers business to you with a personalized thank-you card, phone call, discounts, flowers, dinner, or even a commission.
- Thank your reliable suppliers with a letter and increased orders.
- People will remember your kindness.

19. Provide Business Cards for All Employees

- Should counter people have their own business cards? Drivers? Yes. They're important enough for this tiny investment.
- They'll be proud to leave their cards with every customer and every prospect.
- They'll use the card with friends and relatives, and your name will be in many more places.
- Make employee business cards a type of a coupon whereby employees get something special each time a customer presents their card.

20. Do What the Winners Do

- Is there a company you admire? Analyze its marketing strategies and objectives.

- Adopt the ones you can use, and improve on them.

- Use what works. Collect advertising that attracts your attention and adapt it to your business.

21. Throw a Party

- Invite clients and friends to your home-based business or store, serve refreshments, and plan an interesting demonstration of your product or service.

- At the event, make it *easy* for customers to buy or order your products or services. Accept credit cards and checks, simplify complicated credit forms, and so forth.

- Alert the media. Let the business editor know something special is happening. The media love to cover the unveiling of interesting new products.

- Be friendly and outgoing. If this is not your personality, ask a friend to be a greeter.

22. Give a Gift

- Offer a specialty item that's useful enough to save and that also serves as a reminder of your business (letter opener, coffee mug, paperweight, etc.). Look in the yellow pages under novelties.

23. Three Secrets of Marketing

- *Be committed.* Commit the money and leave it alone. Plant the seeds that will grow later.

- *Be consistent.* Why does McDonald's advertise every day on every channel? Is there anyone in the United States who hasn't heard of McDonald's? The marketing message must be constantly reinforced. Your customers will forget you if they don't hear from you.

- *Be patient*. Most marketing plans take at least 60 days to produce even minimum results. Your efforts will pay off in the long run.

24. Don't Try to Make Money

- Offer customers genuinely useful products or services that make you and your customers happy.
- Do what you love, and the money will follow.

25. Establish a Board of Champions

Every quarter or so, put a dozen of these advisers (friends, family, and business associates whose opinions and judgment you value) in a room and allow them to critique every aspect of your business. For the cost of a nice lunch, this board of advisers can give you a different look at yourself.

Don't be thin-skinned; they may be hard on you or your product, but that's the purpose. They may see problems that you don't. Grow from the experience.

26. Use a Dipstick Now and Then

When explaining your product or service to customers, stop every 30 to 45 seconds and ask a question to see if your message is being received. If they ask you to continue or ask to take notes, you know you're on the right track.

You can't sell it if your message is not being received.

27. Never Assume

Never assume that the customer:

- Can't afford it.
- Won't buy it.
- Doesn't understand the product.
- Won't buy more than one.
- Won't price your competitors.
- Won't like you.

On the other hand, don't assume the opposite is true, either. Just have confidence in your product or service and the need it fills.

28. *Take Little Bites*

- Eskimos eat whales, and tiny termites eat mighty houses the same way—a bite at a time.

- Starting a company, or introducing a new product, is a monumental task if you approach it as a done deal. General Motors didn't start at its present size; its doors opened on the first day of business with no customers, just like yours.

- Good management, a good product properly positioned, and a "never give up" attitude.

- Even with small bites, the meal may become more than you can swallow.

Note: In the September 1992 issue of *Success* magazine is the story of Herb Vest. He started a company that was against accounting regulations in every state. He financed his business with personal credit cards. At one time he was $400,000 in debt and judgments were filed against him. The bank repossessed his car. But he never gave up. "I always knew I'd succeed," he said. Nine years later, nine states had changed the rules and Vest was CEO of a $36 million company. This is the kind of determination, drive, and attitude it takes to be successful. Do you have that kind of determination, drive, and attitude?

29. *Use the Public Library*

- The library has more information on business than anyone can possibly read.

- The librarians will research and find the information you need— a real time-saver.

- Look the books over for two weeks and buy the ones you want to add to your business library.

30. *Use One Medium to Direct Your Customer to Another*

- If the best way to reach your target market (e.g., teens) is with radio, but you have a long story to tell, use your radio spot to tell them about your big sale ad in the newspaper.

31. *Invite Complaints about Your Business or Product*

- Make it easy for your customers to complain about your business. Call them after the sale. Send a postcard asking, "Was everything okay?" "How are we doing?" and so on.

- If your product has a problem, how will you know about it? Isn't it better to get complaint feedback right away rather than waiting until you have hundreds of unhappy customers?

32. *The 100 Percent Perfect Problem (or the 90 Percent Done Problem)*

- If you continue to work on an ad, brochure, or mailer long enough, will you eventually get it perfect? No.

- The reality is that no communications project is ever more than 90 percent perfect. There's always something that could be revised and improved.

- It is better to accept a 90 percent perfect project and let it begin to do its work, rather than keeping it caged while chasing the elusive 100 percent perfect goal.

- If you have a new business or product, the important thing is getting some kind of message out there. You need customers or clients, and you need them fast. Every day you delay, the better chance your competition has to reach your customers. Your materials will go through several evolutionary changes over the years, and you will never be totally happy with them.

33. *Start a Swipe File*   A swipe file is a collection of ads and brochures that copywriters and artists collect or swipe from others for those times when they are stumped for a good idea. Pay attention to any advertising materials that cross your desk. Look at color, type of paper, type styles, types of folding, use of pictures, and phrases used to describe the product or service. What techniques stand out that you could use in your advertising materials?

34. *It's Important to Us, So It Must Be Important to Our Customers*

- Just because issues are important within an organization does not mean they automatically have relevance to your customers.
- This is a by-product of fuzzy thinking, and the problem usually points to managers who lack experience.
- When you consider any project, look at it from the customers' point of view, not the company's. The rule is: "Take care of the customers, and they will take care of the company."

35. *Give Your Customers More Than They Expected*

- Top-quality service does not have to be expensive. Just addressing customers by name might be enough to impress them.
- What small thing can you do for your customers that will surprise them without additional cost to the company?
- Good service generally goes unnoticed and does not receive a comment. Exceptional service does get noticed; so does exceptionally poor service.

Note: Avoid the customer service trap of trying to be all things to all people. You should provide a level of service that you can maintain consistently and profitably. Don't try to wow them. If you do, how are you going to wow them the next time and the time after that?

36. *Use Suppliers and Vendors for Information* Talk to suppliers and salespeople who call on you; they know more about your competition than anyone else. Sometimes in the course of casual conversation they may unknowingly give you important information about your competitor's future plans. If your competition is a public company, buy stock. As a stockholder you will receive all of its annual and quarterly reports.

37. *Pay Attention to People with Disabilities* People with disabilities are becoming a big market. If you can serve some subgroup of that market effectively, you may be able to capture a loyal and lucrative customer base.

38. *Know the Demographics of Your Sales Area* Find out the demographic breakdown of the area you live in or plan on servicing. How many whites, blacks, Hispanics, and so forth are there? What are their income levels? What is the number of homeowners? This is important information, because if the area can't afford or doesn't want your product, then you're out of business before you even start.

Demographic information is available from many sources (these are not the only ones):

- Local newspapers (ask for an advertising rate kit).
- Local chamber of commerce.
- City planning commission.
- Public library (ask the librarian for assistance).
- Local TV and radio stations.

  For more, see the U.S. Census Bureau at www.census.gov.

39. *Subscribe to Industry Magazines*
- Keep up with changing events in your industry by subscribing to trade magazines.

- Lists of all available magazines can be found at the library.
- Many of these magazines do surveys of their subscribers that answer questions such as:
  - How much should I spend on marketing, advertising, insurance, and so on each year?
  - How much should I charge for my product?
  - What age group buys the largest amount(s) of my product?
  - What is the most successful advertising medium to promote my product—TV, radio, direct mail?

For more information, look for *Ulrich's Periodicals Directory* at your local library.

40. Subscribe to Magazines That Can Help Your Business Self-Esteem No matter what the state of the economy is, people are always starting businesses and are still running successful businesses every day of the year. Look for magazines that deal with positive business messages. There are plenty of them out there. Here are three to start with:

1. *Fast Company*—positive messages to keep your spirits up.
2. *Inc.*—the magazine for growing companies.
3. *Entrepreneur*—the small business authority.

These are available at most grocery stores, newsstands, and libraries.

41. Join Organizations That Can Help You Most industries have organizations that support that industry. For example, your local video store may be a member of the Video Software Dealers Association (VSDA).

Where we can find a list of these organizations? The library, perhaps.

Talking to people in the same industry can give you a good idea of what to try and not try in business promotion. There is always someone at these meetings who can help you succeed. These organizations exist to benefit you and your business or product.

Many organizations have conventions that are closed to the general public. The Video Software Dealers Association holds one of the largest conventions in Las Vegas every year (sorry, video dealers only). Conventions are a gold mine of good information.

42. What If I Can't Match a Competitor's Offer? If your competitor is offering 50 percent off over a four-day weekend and you can't afford the extra inventory, or the markdown for that long, what can you do?

You can offer a better deal for a shorter time. Try offering 60 percent off on Saturday morning only. That way, you will drain off a lot of your competitor's customers on a busy sale day, and you will be perceived as a better place to do business. To make up some of your losses, sell higher-margin add-on products.

43. Track Your Clients' Special Needs Create a form to keep track of clients' requests for special services and products and whether you can meet these requests. By studying these forms periodically, you can track interest in new products or services that you should offer.

44. Make Sure Your Clients Can Reach You

- Print your company name, address, web site, e-mail, and phone and fax numbers on all materials, including packing slips and invoices.
- Provide customers with business cards and brochures containing all contact information.

- Remember, customers who have to search for your number may come across your competitor's number first.

45. *Learn More about Your Customers*   Learn more about customers than just the business they're in. Pay attention to local newspapers and let customers know you read about them.

46. *Be an Expert*

- Offer seminars, establishing your company as an expert on the subject.
- Seminars help cement relations with current customers, attract prospects, and increase your company's exposure.
- Choose a topic with broad appeal for your client and prospect base.
- Follow up with attendees by mail or in person.

47. *Write Sales Letters*

- With e-mail, fax machines, and cellular phones, most of us don't write letters anymore. But they are an effective means of communication and, unlike phone calls, almost always reach the intended audience.
- Letters enhance a company's professional image, help avoid misunderstandings, and often make a sale.
- Write letters explaining your company's services, detailing how your company helped another well-known client or thanking a customer for an order. Handwrite "Personal" on the outside for better response.
- Keep a library of well-written letters for employees to use as models.

48. *Listen to Your Customers*   Pay attention to questions new customers ask. They may be telling you about an unpleasant experience they had with a previous company if they ask about service, exchanges, return policies, and so on. Have an employee meeting and go over some of the phrases that might be red flags to watch for. Armed with that knowledge, you can let these customers know that you will solve their problem with no hassles.

49. Use Personalized Post-It Notes to Promote Your Company

- Every office uses these little sticky notes, and they stick them to everything. With personalized Post-it Notes, everyone from the CEO to the receptionist will see your company name almost every day.

- If they have a problem you can solve, your name and number are right there, stuck to the page.

50. Rate Your Customers for Surprising Results

- Assign customers a category such as A, B, C, D, and so forth based on several criteria. Include profitability and time spent handling orders and special requests.

- You'll quickly realize that some high-volume accounts are not contributing significantly to the bottom line.

- Develop a plan to inform all employees who the most profitable customers are and who should receive the best efforts of the company.

51. Know That Marketing Is Not a Battle of Products; It's a Battle of Perceptions

- Campbell's soup is number one in the United States but not in the United Kingdom.

- Heinz soup is number one in the United Kingdom but not in the United States.

- It's a matter of perception. Would we buy Pennzoil cake mix? Why not? Because we perceive Pennzoil to be motor oil, not cake mix. Even if Pennzoil made the best cake mix in the world, it would still be a very tough sell to most people.

52. *Ignore the Competition* Too many people worry so much about their competitors that they forget what they are doing. If you're confident in your vision, don't worry about your competition.

53. *Be Tenacious in Your Vision* Don't be discouraged by setbacks. They aren't failures. Failure is simply failing to persevere. Whatever you are doing, if you are getting any kind of results, persevere.

54. *Tips for Successful Magazine Advertising (Also See #55)*

- A two-page spread attracts about one-quarter more readers than a one-page ad.
- A full-page ad attracts one-third more readers than a half-page ad.
- People respond better to illustrations or photos showing the product in use than to those that show the product just sitting there.
- Ads with people in them attract more attention than those without.

55. *Is Bigger Better?*

- Should you use your limited advertising budget to create larger, more visible ads that restrict you to advertising less frequently, or smaller, less visible ads that you can then afford to run more frequently?
- The answer: Run smaller ads more frequently. Most people, even those who are likely candidates for your products, typically don't respond to ads the first time they see them, no matter how large they are.
- Prospects may need to see the ad a number of times before they take action.

56. Understand That When Emotion and Reason Conflict, Emotion Always Wins!   Although people like to believe they react rationally to products, offers, and the like, the truth is they react emotionally and then look for a rationale to confirm their decision. So, the smart marketer will acknowledge the motivator and the need to rationalize in presenting a product or an offer. Have you ever bought a CD just to get one song? Have you ever considered the color when buying a car? Is that logical?

57. Look outside Your Industry for Best-in-Class Examples   What firm has the best billing system? The best sales force? The best customer service? If you measure yourself only versus your competition, you'll be only as good or a little better than they are. But is that who you're competing against? No. Your customer is experiencing those best-in-class processes from someone, and they are measuring your delivery against that someone's delivery.

58. Heed the Two Basic Tenets of Selling

1. People buy from other people more happily than from faceless corporations.

2. In the marketplace, as in the theater, there is indeed a factor at work called the willing suspension of disbelief. Who stands behind our pancakes? Aunt Jemima. Our angel food cakes? Betty Crocker. Our coffee? Juan Valdez. It's all myth, but the myths are comforting.

59. Get the Second Order   The most important order you ever get from a customer is the second order.

Why? Because a two-time buyer is twice as likely to buy again as a one-time buyer.

60. Catalog Rule #1—Best Seller in the Upper Left?   Turn the page of any catalog, and the first thing you look at is the upper left-hand corner of the spread. That's where to place your best seller, your bread and butter, right? Well, what if your best seller is a visual dog? What if, for instance, your mainstay is a pair of black shoes? Then kill the rule, and raise another flag. Put a pair of wild socks in the upper left for stopping power, and direct your reader to the old tried-and-true best seller elsewhere on the spread.

61. *Know Your Audience; Then Write to One Member*   Don't address the sea of 500,000 nameless and faceless people who will receive your information. In your ads, brochures, mailings, and so on, pick one customer you know and like and write the copy to that one individual as though you were sitting down and having a conversation about your business.

62. *Get on the Ball*   Be ready to be where your customer wants you, when your customer wants you, with what your customer wants. Just-in-time marketing is crucial, as 24-hour, seven-day, customized products and services spoil people.

63. *Beware of the Negative*   Make sure you deal with all your customers in good faith and with integrity. Negative word of mouth, especially on community bulletin boards and the Internet, can cripple your business more than positive public relations can help it.

64. *Focus on the Smaller Market*   For every trend, there is at least one countertrend. It's sometimes better to focus on a smaller market—one nobody is serving because they're all off catering to the bigger trend.

65. *Use Direct Mail*   Pick up any business book, by any author, and you'll find that there is no other way to sell a product that is cheaper and more successful than direct mail. Forty-six percent of Americans have purchased something by direct mail. If you think of it as junk mail, think again. It's solid gold mail.

Here's a simplified version of how it works:

- A full-page ad in *Time* magazine costs approximately $80,000 to $90,000 and reaches two million people.

- However, not all of the two million readers of *Time* have a need for our product. These people go right past our ad without a second thought. The money we've spent to reach them is wasted.

- What if we could have two pages, three pages, or 11 pages to tell our story? Could you tell the story of your product on 11 pages?

- Wouldn't it be nice if we could have our 11-page ad delivered to only the *Time* subscribers who were interested in our product?

- The answer: direct mail, using a mailing list of people who should buy our product based on our product position and their past buying behavior. If we sell baby products, wouldn't a mailing list of prospective new mothers be nice? How about first-time mothers?

- Now we can send our 11-page ad for substantially less than the *Time* ad, we don't have to compete with other ads in the same magazine, and our message is reaching a target audience that has demonstrated that they have a definite need for our product and a history of buying it.

66. *Use Newspaper Specials* Each year newspapers create special inserts or sections on topics of local interest: bridal fairs, real estate home shows, craft fairs, and so on. These sections usually have a larger readership than the regular newspaper, and your ad can generate more business. Note: Look at last year's edition and check with advertisers to see if the response was worth going into these sections. In many small towns, it is.

67. *Select Newspaper Placement* Where your ad appears in the paper can have a dramatic impact on how successful it will be. Many people, even if they don't believe in astrology, read their daily horoscope. Depending on your product, being near the horoscopes will increase your ad's exposure.

68. *Obtain Professional Newspaper Ad Design* When running newspaper and/or magazine ads, the salesperson will sometimes recommend they do the design of your ad as a money-saving option. This is usually a bad idea—not because they can't do it or don't have the ability, but because their designers are under a deadline to create many ads in a short amount of time. In most cases your ad won't receive the care and attention to detail it deserves because of the time constraints.

If you doubt this, pick up almost any newspaper and proofread the ads or look for corrections and retractions of past incorrect ads. Even though it may cost a little more, have a professional design your ads.

69. *Save with the Professional Designer* When doing newspaper or magazine ads, have your designer create individual pieces for your advertising. Separate logo, text, pictures, and graphics for upcoming events, so they can be quickly combined for a quick ad when needed. You pay one fee for all the pieces and assemble the pieces needed for each ad you place.

70. *Remember These Tips When Using Photos in the Newspaper*

- Make sure the photos are not too dark or too light.
- Take the photos to a print shop and have the printer scan them and adjust color and brightness and correct any defects. If the photos are similar in lightness and darkness, the printer can gang them together for one scan.

- If you need to make a head shot for the newspaper, ask the photographer to use a light background instead of a gray or black background. Your photo will show up much better in the black-and-white newspaper.

- If you're using photos of your building, keep in mind the image you want to project to the reader. Does your business look open, not closed? Are there cars in the parking lot? Does the business look prosperous?

- If you are using a photo of your employees, the common mistake is to take the photo from too far away. For some reason, people feel the shot must include each person's full body, and as a consequence the faces of the employees are unclear. Arrange your employees in two or three rows, with those in back standing on curbs or boxes. Move in so the bottom of the picture hits the front row of employees about chest high. This way the reader can clearly see everyone's face, and the ad will be much more effective.

71. *Look like News in the Newspaper* Make your ad look like a news story, complete with headlines and columns. This is often referred to as an editorial ad. The newspaper will require the word "Advertisement" at the top of your ad, but if you use a catchy headline and an attention-grabbing first paragraph, people will quickly forget they are reading an ad.

72. *Advertise in Service and Home-Based Business Directories*
Many small town newspapers have a service or business directory section. This is the section people often turn to for plumbers, landscapers, electricians, and computer help. Check rates; you may be able to run a larger ad more often at a lower price.

73. *Use SCAN Ads* Every state has a state newspaper association that offers Suburban Classified Ad Network (SCAN) ads. A SCAN ad is a small classified ad that is placed once with a member newspaper and then appears in hundreds of newspapers in that state. For example, in Montana, SCAN ads cost a few hundred dollars to run in 100 to 120 state and local papers. In California, SCAN ads are more expensive, but appear in papers with an estimated readership of several million people.

74. Use the Service Organizations You Belong To   When news of your business is published, be sure to send a copy to any trade organizations you belong to so they can include the news in their magazines or newsletters.

75. Say Thanks for the Memory   If you do get an article printed about your business, be sure to send a thank-you card or letter to the reporter. Let the reporter know you would be pleased to be a source for any future articles on your subject.

76. Point Out That There Are Two Sides to Any Story   If a newspaper prints a negative story regarding your business or industry, immediately prepare a press release that shows the positive side of the story. If the topic is controversial, your press release may spark a positive article, with your company portrayed in a more positive light.

77. Remember There's More Than One Paper   Just because you're in a small town doesn't mean your local town paper is the only print option. Many people and businesses subscribe to newspapers from larger cities in your state. In Bozeman, Montana, we have the *Bozeman Chronicle*, but many people also subscribe to the *Billings Gazette*. If you're doing business throughout the state, this may be a better advertising option. Get the subscription numbers for all the papers delivered in your area. The larger ones may be more economical and reach more customers than the local paper.

78. *Walk a Mile in My Shoes*   Reporters often have no idea what your average workday is like, or how your business works. Invite them to spend the day or part of a day with you, so they can write the story from actual firsthand observation.

79. *Make It Easy*   Most of us want our lives to be easier and less complicated. If your product or service saves time or makes life easier, that may be more important to some customers than saving money. For example, cheese, sliced and individually wrapped in cellophane, costs more money. Imagine the first response to that idea: "Nobody's too lazy to slice their own cheese. It'll never sell." But it did, and still does.

80. *Provide Weekly Information*   Contact your local radio station if you have daily or weekly information people need. We live in ski country, and three different resort areas deliver snow reports on all the radio stations. A stockbroker reports on the market numbers daily.

Tips for Success on the Internet

81. *Think Your Customers Only Use the Web for Big Ticket Items?*
Guess again. Your customers are using the net for a wide variety of reasons that you can capitalize on. Consider the following DigCon Study (Source: www.avenuearazorfish.com/reports/DigConsStudy.pdf).

When you are in the market for a product that costs $100.00 or less what determines if you will use the web to help make purchase decisions? Please select which answer best matches your behavior.

- 1% I never use the web when making purchasing decisions for items less than $100
- 17% I use the web if I think that prices will vary by retailer

- 18% I use the web if I want to compare products and features
- 5% I use the web if I want to locate retailers
- 20% I use the web to read online reviews and ratings of products or brands
- 39% I use the web to research products and features

Where would you most likely begin your web search for this product?

- 54% I would use a general search engine to see what comes up
- 14% I would use comparison shopping search engines since I want to see the price up front
- 15% I would visit a specific eCommerce site that I frequent or that I think specializes in that type of product
- 15% I would visit the website of a known and established retail store
- 1% Other
- 1% No Answer

82. *Value Online Researchers* Users may go off-line to ring up high-ticket sales, but the Web is where they make up their minds. These people are not just window shoppers.

- Seventy-one percent bought at least one high-ticket item they researched online (up from 46 percent the previous year).
- Seventy-nine percent shopped for computer products; 46 percent purchased retail.
- Seventy percent researched airline ticket prices, hotels, or car rentals; 46 percent made reservations off-line.
- Forty-four percent shopped for a car; 26 percent bought off-line.

83. *Make Your Page Fast*   More and more people are moving to high-speed Internet, which will allow you to use movies and music to tell your story.

84. *Understand Why Customers Go to Web Sites*   A site map is a single page that displays all the links on your site in one place. To make it easier to navigate, divide the links into categories with related links as subcategories. Search engines love site maps, and they will follow all your links as they catalog your site and give your site a higher ranking.

85. *Don't Overdo the Technology*   Don't let hipper-than-thou web site builders throw your marketing know-how out the window. Bells and whistles are fine for some products, but customers are looking for a fast, simple solution to their needs and desires. Make it as simple and as easy as possible for them to use your site. If you can add extra features without compromising ease of navigation, feel free.

86. *Enhance Your Image*   Provide valuable added extras that will enhance your image as the industry leader.

Make your site a must-visit for the latest breaking news, and update it frequently. If there are no new products lined up, provide industry updates, gossip, trends, and forecasts. This will bring visitors back and motivate them to spread the word on the Internet grapevine.

87. *Use Banners and Links to Get Noticed*

- How do you get folks to use your banner? Include the words "Click Here"; this is a psychological call to action.
- A Netsmart survey found 41 percent of users discover new sites through banners and links.

88. *Put Your Web Site Address Everywhere*　Your web site address should be on every piece of material your customer will see: business cards, brochures, postcards, flyers, ads, signs, and delivery vehicles. Consider a tattoo? Well, let's not go overboard.

89. *Animate Your Ad*　In evaluating the performance of some 30 ads over a series of months, ZDNet of Cambridge, Massachusetts, found that animated ads generated click-through rates at least 15 percent higher than static ads, and in some cases as much as 40 percent higher.

90. *Copyright Your Web Page*　Make sure you include a copyright line (©2008 Your Name) on all your web pages. This will protect you if some one else decides to download some of your graphics and use them on their site. The Web is protected just like any other visual publication.

91. *Register with Search Engines*　Register your web site with as many search engines as possible. In fact, do a search on search engines. You will find several hundred. The largest one, Google (www.google.com), as well as Yahoo! (www.yahoo.com), will register your site by contacting them at their sites. Also consider adding your site to www.dmoz.com, which is one of the largest directories on the Web. Make sure you follow its instructions to the letter when adding your site. Dmoz is very particular.

One other important point: You can't rely completely on search engines to publicize your web site. You must advertise it whenever and wherever you can. Business cards, brochures, and all your advertising must include your web site address. I had a sign made for the rear window of my automobile with my web site address, www.smalltownmarketing.com.

Learn about search engines at: www.searchenginewatch.com.

92. Spell Out Terms and Conditions If you are going to sell or market products on the Web, it is important that your site have certain legal positions spelled out in legal language. These are the terms and conditions (Ts and Cs).

For example, you may want to notify customers about your site security if you are using credit cards: What actions are you liable for, and what are the risks the customer takes? Spelling these out in advance and posting them as part of your site can head off legal problems down the road.

93. Include a Guest Book When people visit your site, ask them to sign your guest book. Why? Here are a few reasons:

- *Demographics*. What cities and countries are your hits coming from?
- *Future advertising on your site*. If you know the demographics of your site, you can then provide this information to other companies that may pay you to post a banner on your page or a link to their page.
- *Tracking*. Keep track of frequent customers and big spenders and ask if you can e-mail them with any special sales or promotions you have planned.

94. Update Your Site Often The only reason people return to sites is for new information. People will stop returning to a site after a few times if there is no new information. Update weekly (daily if possible), and be sure to note on the first page the date of the update.

95. Use Ads and Banners Before you decide to place an ad or banner on another web site, monitor the site for about a month. Look for changes and how often the site is updated. If the site has nothing new to offer, the traffic will slow and your ad will become ineffective.

96. Check Online Publications   Many publications, like *Time* and *Newsweek*, have an online presence. See if your industry publications have web sites, and if so check the sites for past articles on your business or industry. Contact them via e-mail about your site, and ask if you can submit articles for their publications.

97. Observe Holidays and Special Events on the Web   Change your pages to reflect what's going on in the world. At Christmastime, decorate your web site just like you would decorate your own storefront. The nice thing about this is that once you've created the decorations they can be reused year after year.

98. Surf the Web   Start setting aside time to surf the Web for pages about your industry and to see who is linked to whom and where the links go. What you're looking for is a community of sites within your industry that have linked together for the good of all. Once you find them, see if you can join the community.

99. Expect Criticism and Welcome It   Criticism will come from those who want you to improve your site. Don't take it personally. Treat it as valuable research and listen to the majority. If you don't fill the void for these visitors, they will stop coming to your site. Expect feedback and welcome it.

100. Protect Your Intellectual Property   Intellectual property on the Internet is defined as software, patents, books, videos, music, photographs, trademarks, fictional characters, copyrights, and web pages. Protect your web site and the information there.

Keep in mind that copyrights don't apply to ideas or ways of doing things. An excellent example of this is clumping cat litter. The guy who invented clumping cat litter just had a good idea that he couldn't protect. Pet supply companies called down to research and development and asked how many formulas they could use to make clumping cat litter. The answer was maybe 10,000 different kinds of ingredients and formulas.

Last but Not Least

101. *Don't Forget the Kids*   There may be times when you have a special project that requires temporary help: a cleanup campaign, an in-house mailing, or help moving the business to another location. Instead of hiring part-time workers from a temp agency, check the local high school or university. There are always groups of responsible and dependable young people who are raising money for some school project. When you do this, two things happen:

1. No payroll taxes.
2. A tax-deductible donation for your business (check the cause and with your accountant).

102. *Sponsor Teams*   One great way to get involved in the community is to sponsor a sports team. The parents of the team members will certainly frequent your business. We have a local hockey team that's doing well, and many businesses associate themselves with the team. Don't forget to add your web site address on any team literature or signage.

103. *Hire Part-Timers for Uneven Workloads*   Many businesses become very busy at certain times of the year. Sometimes they find they have too many full-time employees. Consider hiring part-timers at higher pay for fewer hours. You will save money by not having to pay benefits to part-timers, and you can get by with fewer full-time employees. You may find yourself with higher-quality part-timers who will stay with you longer.

104. Make Sure Employees See the Big Picture   It's hard for small, growing companies to pay people as much as some larger companies might pay. The cost of insurance and other benefits is high, and employees usually don't understand the expense of keeping them on the payroll. When you hire employees, make sure they know the score. If their base salary is $25,000, let them know that with insurance and benefits the total package may be $36,750. (When raises come around, there may be a 4 percent salary increase and a 7 percent increase in benefits.) This way the employee is more in touch with the actual earnings and the sacrifice made by the company.

105. If They Helped, Pay 'Em   Many companies seem to feel that they shouldn't pay any type of bonus to part-time employees. Keep in mind that these folks helped with customers, production, and delivery, and they talk about your business in their private everyday lives. If they're on your payroll, they are necessary and should be made to feel so.

106. Offer a Student Bonus   Tie salaries to grade point average for high school and college students you hire. Give a progressive bonus if the student excels in the classroom. In most cases you will find more responsible and disciplined workers who will enhance your business.

107. Respect Your Customers' Time
- E-mail first.
- Fax second.
- Phone, your third and last resort.

Customers are busy, too. Their time is valuable. Most will read the e-mails and look at the faxes in a timely manner. Be patient.

108. *Offer Special Deals to Special Customers*   Each day, call five of your best customers, and offer them a special deal that is only for them and only today. They may not buy, but we all like to know we can get something special that someone else can't.

109. *Use a Motto*   "Winston tastes good . . ." Can you fill in the rest? Most people can: ". . . like a cigarette should!" That campaign hasn't been used in 35 years, but it's still remembered as a powerful advertising message. "When you care enough to send the very best." Hallmark has used this motto for years and has made sending Hallmark cards a measure of the recipient's importance.

110. *Create a Bulk Mailing Package*   If your business is located on a busy downtown street, contact all the businesses on your block and see if they would be willing to package a postcard ad campaign with you.

Five or 10 businesses would send postcard packages by bulk mail and share the mailing cost, which would be cheaper than each store mailing out its own individual postcards. Realize additional savings by sharing printing costs by gang printing all the postcards together at the printer.

111. *Use Last Year for This Year*   If you've been in business for a year, you have some idea of what to expect in year two. Use last year's information to plan this year. If you have five years it's even better. Keep in mind that business forecasting is like the weather. Just because there was a storm on this day last year doesn't mean it will happen again this year.

112. *Employ a Five and Ten Philosophy*   Every business day, try to contact 10 new customers or clients. From the 10, try to get at least five referrals of other potential customers to contact. That way you will never run out of potential customers.

113. *Look How We Did It* If your business solves people's or companies' problems, use customer testimonials for a powerful advertising tool. Solicit letters from customers who used your service or product and found that their lives are better for it.

When companies are reluctant or won't take the time to do this, I sometimes offer to write the letter myself and have them okay the wording and sign it. Many customers are so pleased with your service they will often agree to do this for you.

114. *Have an Advisory Board* If you have created your board of champions (see tip 25), ask them to allow you to use their names on your stationery as an advisory board. This will give your business a certain amount of credibility.

Is Your Tip #115? This is a small cross-section sample of some successful ideas that clients, magazines, books, business associates, and customers have passed on to me over the years.

SOME FINAL THOUGHTS

Well, congratulations! You've persevered to the very end. It's that kind of resolve that makes successful people who they are. If I have any last words of encouragement, they might be a quote from one of my favorite books, *Think and Grow Rich*, by Napoleon Hill (Ballantine Books, 1996; orig. pub. 1937; abr. ed. 1960).

Hill claims, "Every adversity, every failure, and every heartache carries with it the SEED of an equivalent or GREATER BENEFIT." In other words, build on your mistakes. Measure, improve, and grow, and you will be unstoppable.

Thanks for taking the time to read this book. I sincerely hope the tips and ideas I've presented will help you build a successful and profitable business.

I'd really like to hear about your business successes and challenges.

E-mail me at tommail@smalltownmarketing.com.

Visit the Small Town Marketing.Com web site at www.smalltown marketing.com.

Or write to:

Tom Egelhoff
Small Town Marketing
P.O. Box 271
Bozeman, MT 59771-0271

INDEX